First Certificate Masterclass

Teacher's Book

Jenny Quintana

Simon Haines

Barbara Stewart

OXFORD

UNIVERSITY PRESS

OXFORD

UNIVERSITY PRESS

Great Clarendon Street, Oxford OX2 6DP

Oxford University Press is a department of the University of Oxford.
It furthers the University's objective of excellence in research, scholarship,
and education by publishing worldwide in

Oxford New York

Auckland Cape Town Dar es Salaam Hong Kong Karachi
Kuala Lumpur Madrid Melbourne Mexico City Nairobi
New Delhi Shanghai Taipei Toronto

With offices in

Argentina Austria Brazil Chile Czech Republic France Greece
Guatemala Hungary Italy Japan Poland Portugal Singapore
South Korea Switzerland Thailand Turkey Ukraine Vietnam

OXFORD and OXFORD ENGLISH are registered trade marks of
Oxford University Press in the UK and in certain other countries

Printed in Spain by Unigraf S.L.

ACKNOWLEDGEMENTS

The authors and publishers would like to thank: Petrina Cliff, Thorkild Gantner,
Vicky McWilliam, Garth Cadden, and the First Certificate students of St Giles
International, London Central.

The publisher is grateful to the University of Cambridge Local Examinations
Syndicate for permission to reproduce FCE answer sheets.

Contents

Student's Book Contents

Introduction

Target users

First Certificate Masterclass is an upper intermediate course aimed at students preparing for the Cambridge First Certificate in English examination. It can also be used by upper intermediate students following general English courses. The material in the course is all at FCE level.

Student's Book

The *First Certificate Masterclass* Student's Book consists of twelve units, each based on a different topic. Each unit consists of the following sections: Introduction, Reading, Grammar and Practice, Vocabulary, Listening, Speaking, Writing and Overview. The first seven units also contain Exam Techniques sections.

While it is anticipated that the units will generally be used in consecutive order, this is not essential, as there is no fixed grammatical or lexical progression. It is important that the sections within units are done in sequence, as grammar and vocabulary are taken from previous texts or recordings.

In addition to introducing and practising the skills which students will need to perform well in the exam, the course functions as a general coursebook which introduces, studies and practises key aspects of grammar and vocabulary.

Introduction

This section presents the overall theme of the unit by engaging students' interest in the new topics, activating general knowledge of them, introducing related vocabulary and providing opportunities for both general fluency practice and specific exam practice for Paper 5 Speaking.

Reading

All the reading passages are authentic texts, with only minimum modifications within the guidelines for the exam. They have been selected from a variety of sources – magazines, journals, popular and serious newspapers – and reflect a variety of registers and styles, ranging from formal to informal and serious to humorous.

Each task type in FCE Paper 1 is practised three times, including an Exam techniques section, where suggestions for approaching each task are made.

Except when it occurs in the Exam techniques section, each reading passage is preceded by *Think ahead*, which contains activities designed to introduce the topic of the reading, and gives students the opportunity to share ideas, knowledge and opinions. Sometimes students are asked to read the text quickly to check their ideas before they do the examination task. This gives them essential practice in skimming a text quickly for gist comprehension or scanning to find specific information.

Before students read the text for more detailed comprehension, you may like to check that they understand key vocabulary contained in it. The *Teacher's Book* includes lists of potentially difficult words and their meanings. However, by the end of the course and in preparation for the examination, we recommend that this is kept to a minimum. Deducing the meaning of unknown words from their context is an important skill which students need to develop.

No guidelines are given on how long students should spend on each reading task. Use your own judgement, allowing more time at the beginning of the course, when students will need extra time to familiarise themselves with the demands of each task type, and less time towards the end to reflect the time available in the exam.

The Reading sections also contain follow-up vocabulary extension exercises, and discussion activities (*Over to You*) related to the topic of the text.

Grammar and practice

Each unit focuses on one major area of grammar. This is related to the Reading or Listening section which precedes it.

In order to exploit what students already know, an inductive approach to grammar has been adopted. This means that the formal rules of grammar are not presented in the first instance, but examples of the target language are given in context. Students answer questions or do a variety of tasks to show what they know or what they can work out for themselves.

It is recommended that students work through these questions and tasks individually or in pairs before checking their answers or ideas with you, or in the *Grammar reference* at the back of the book. However, if students are not very confident about their knowledge of grammar, you may prefer to lead them through the questions and tasks, eliciting answers from individuals and providing correction and clarification where necessary.

The main purpose of the practice exercises which follow the grammar questions and tasks is accuracy, so you should correct students' language where necessary. Some practice exercises are open-ended requiring students to complete sentences with their own ideas. These should also be regarded as accuracy practice and be corrected in detail.

Vocabulary

It is vital for students to extend their vocabulary systematically, and for this reason vocabulary plays a prominent role in every unit. As well as regular contextualised vocabulary work in the Reading and Listening sections, most units contain two vocabulary pages which focus on specific topics or lexical systems. *Exam techniques* related to Paper 3 Use of English tasks may also include a vocabulary focus. Wherever possible, students are encouraged to use vocabulary in controlled and free practice activities. Selected items of vocabulary are also revised in *Overview* sections.

Listening

Each task type in FCE Paper 4 is practised several times, including an Exam techniques section, where suggestions for approaching each task are made.

As in the exam, the recordings are scripted or semi-scripted and there is a variety of accents. Students are given practice in listening for gist, listening for main points, listening for detail or specific information, and deducing meaning.

Listenings are preceded by pre-listening tasks in a *Lead in* and followed by related vocabulary work and opportunities for discussion. The audioscripts are reproduced in each unit of the *Teacher's Book*.

Speaking

Each section begins with a *Lead in*, which introduces the topic and gives students the opportunity to share personal information and opinions. This is followed by practice of a Part 2 task, or a Part 3 and Part 4 task from Paper 5 Speaking, together with Exam tips. All these activities should be done in pairs or small groups and should be treated as opportunities for fluency and examination practice. It is recommended that any correction should be done after students have completed the task.

In Units 1, 4, 6 and 7, students are able to listen to and analyse the performance of real FCE candidates doing similar tasks.

There are many further opportunities for practice of Part 2 and Part 4 task types in Introductions and elsewhere throughout the book.

Writing

The Writing section follows a similar procedure throughout. First, analysis of an example task, which focuses on the features of the task type. Second, practice of a particular aspect of writing, for example: beginnings and endings of articles, connecting ideas, creating interest. Third, *Think, plan, write*, which sets an exam-type task and guides students towards a successful completion of the task.

Each Paper 2 Writing task type is covered at least once, while the set book question is featured in the *Writing Guide*.

Exam advice on writing is an integral part of the *Writing* section of each unit and in the *Writing Guide* at the back of the book.

Overview

This section reviews the grammar and vocabulary practised in the unit. It also gives students further practice in Paper 3 Use of English task types.

Exam Techniques

This section gives advice in the form of a set of *Dos and Don'ts* for each of the task types for Paper 1 Reading, Paper 3 Use of English, and Paper 4 Listening. This is followed by opportunities for practice. The Exam Techniques sections should be used in conjunction with the information about the exam on pages 4–8 of the Student's Book and can be treated as training tasks rather than tests. It is important to encourage the development of ways of approaching different exam task types without the pressure of exam conditions.

Other features

Exam factfile

The *Exam Factfile* provides detailed information about the five papers of the exam. Each task type is listed with a note of the number of items involved, what students have to do and what is being tested. Page references for appropriate *Exam techniques* pages in the book are given.

Over to you

Over to you tasks are included as follow-up activities related to the Reading and Listening sections. Their purpose is to give students opportunities to react personally to the broad topics relating to texts and recordings. They should be regarded as fluency activities which will help students to develop their general speaking skills and can generally be done in pairs or small groups or as whole class activities. Encourage students to discuss topics in a lively interested way for two to three minutes.

Writing guide

The *Writing Guide* at the back of the book consists of exam advice related to each of the task types in Paper 2 Writing. Each guide offers advice under these headings:

How should I approach the task? which contains a sample exam task and connected questions.

How should I structure a formal letter, article, etc.? which contains a model answer to the sample task with notes pointing out key features of the answer.

What phrases can I use? which contains phrases and expressions relevant to each task type.

One section is devoted to the Set book question, which is not practised elsewhere. Four sample exam tasks and two model answers are provided.

Grammar reference

The Grammar reference at the back of the book is organised on a unit-by-unit basis. It contains concise explanations and further examples of the grammar in each unit. This section should be regarded as a first point of reference for students to check their answers to inductive questions and tasks or when working through practice exercises. It can also be used for general revision purposes.

Teacher's Book

The *First Certificate Masterclass Teacher's Book* contains twelve units of notes to accompany the Student's Book. There are procedural notes on how to approach the tasks, complete audioscripts for all recordings with answers highlighted, and further suggestions for *Optional activities*. Answer keys are given, and, where there is no single answer for a task, possible answers have been provided.

At the back of the Teacher's book there is information about www.oxfordenglishtesting.com

Workbook Resource Pack

The *First Certificate Masterclass* Workbook Resource Pack consists of a Workbook of twelve six-page units, each of which covers the following areas: Reading, Listening, Grammar, Vocabulary, Use of English and Writing.

There is a topic link with the corresponding units in the *Student's Book* and practice of grammar and vocabulary from the units. In addition, every unit includes some vocabulary extension. In most units there is a focus on phrasal verbs.

The Writing sections do not require students to produce exam-type answers, the focus being on relevant micro-skills, such as *Titles and opening sentences* (Articles) *Using contrasting expressions* (Discursive Essays), etc.

There is also a MultiROM at the back of the Workbook which contains audio material linked to the listening sections of the Workbook. Students can play the audio in a CD player or on a computer. There is also a link which launches students to www.oxfordenglishtesting.com where they get access to two interactive online FCE practice tests. The tests offer authentic FCE practice, automatic marking for instant results and an online dictionary look-up facility. For further information please see the section about www.oxfordenglishtesting.com at the back of this Teacher's Book or visit the website itself.

Web materials

As a further resource, teachers may download materials from the Internet at www.oup.com/elt/teacher/exams

These are:

Extra activities

One activity per unit which provides extra practice in the vocabulary, grammar or speaking skills which have been introduced. There are also four additional extra activities which practise four main areas of vocabulary covered in the Student's Book: phrasal verbs, prepositions, confusing words, and collocations.

Unit tests

A two-page test for each unit, covering the grammar and vocabulary taught in that unit.

Progress tests

Three tests which review the grammar and vocabulary of the units within the context of FCE Use of English tasks. Test 1 covers Units 1–4, Test 2 covers Units 5–8, and Test 3 covers Units 9–12.

For more information about the FCE Examination, please refer to the Cambridge ESOL First Certificate in English handbook, which can be downloaded from the OUP exams website.

1 The sexes

Introduction p9

1 Possible answer

Photos 3 and 5 are similar because they show men and women together. However, in photo 3 we see a man and woman fulfilling traditional roles – the man is the boss and the woman is the secretary. In photo 5, we see men and women on more equal terms.

2 Possible answer

The photos show that the roles of men and women vary widely in today's society. Each sex is more comfortable taking on some of the roles traditionally associated with the other.

Reading p10

Think ahead

1 Check students understand the meaning of these words: *set sail* (start a journey), *crew* (group of people who work on a ship, aeroplane, spaceship, etc.), *artificial* (non-natural), *interstellar* (amongst the stars).

Check students understand the meaning of the extract by asking these questions: *Who will be on-board the spaceship?* (women only) *Why won't men be required?* (because the women will be able to have children without them) *What is Alpha Centauri?* (It's the star system that is closest to earth.)

2 Possible answer

A single-sex crew might miss the company of the opposite sex and the distractions they can bring.

3 This exercise is intended to encourage students to get to know the text before the main reading task. Do not allow them to spend too much time on it.

Possible answer

In the text, John Moore thinks mixed-sex crews could have families which would make space travel easier to tolerate.

Multiple choice

4 This exercise involves reading in detail, so allow plenty of time for it. Before they begin, make sure students understand the rubric and the multiple-choice questions. You may like to check that the students understand the meaning of these words: *tensions* (bad feelings between people), *remote* (distant/isolated), *accomplish* (finish), *colonisation* (when a group of people settle in a new area), *constraint* (restriction), *adjust to* (become accustomed to), *sustain* (keep going), *monogamy* (the practice of having only one wife or husband over a period of time), *morals* (ethics/socially acceptable ideas), *far-fetched* (unlikely).

Key

1 C	4 A
2 D	5 B
3 C	

Over to you

Over to you sections are intended to offer practice in speaking skills by allowing students to express their opinions about the topic of a section of the unit. The questions can be asked directly to your class and used as the basis of a class discussion, or students could be asked to discuss the questions in pairs or small groups.

Possible answers

Suitable people: doctors, nurses, midwives, teachers, builders, farmers, scientists, etc.

Personal qualities: determination, bravery, sense of adventure, sense of humour, ability to work as a team, etc.

Group nouns

5 Key

a class

b jury

c team

d staff

e audience

f crowd

Examples of other group nouns: family, group, orchestra, couple.

Grammar and practice p12

The future

1 After students have completed the task, encourage them to refer to the Grammar reference on page 174.

Key

a 4

b 1

c 5

d 7

e 6

f 3

g 2

2 Encourage students to read through any text before beginning a task. In this case, ask them to read the text quickly, ignoring the gaps. Check they understand by asking these questions: *Where are Sue and her friends planning to travel to?* (Paris) *What are they going to do there?* (go to a rock concert)

Key

1 break up

2 're having

3 're starting

4 're going to get up

5 leaves

6 'll stop

7 're going to drive

8 will take

9 'll probably go

10 're going to catch

11 'll send

12 Are you doing

3 Possible answers

a I'm going to ask them to tell the truth.

b I'm afraid I'm visiting relatives in the holidays.

c I'll put up the decorations and I'll select some music, if you like.

d I'll be twenty-one.

e I'll probably be married.

f Tomorrow is going to be icy.

Future continuous and future perfect

4 After students have completed the task, encourage them to refer to the Grammar reference on page 174.

Key

a 2

b 3

c 1

5 Possible answers

a This time next week I'll be *sitting on the beach.*

b By this time next year I'll have *finished my exams.*

c This time next year I'll be *living in Spain.*

d In five years' time I'll have *started my own company.*

Cloze

6 Ask students to read the text quickly, ignoring the gaps. Check they understand by asking these questions: *In which country is the language spoken?* (China) *Why is it unusual?* (It's believed to be the only women's language in the world.) *Why is it becoming extinct?* (The women who speak it are dying and nobody new is learning it.)

Key

1 by

2 is

3 on

4 been

5 to

6 far

7 who

8 are

9 still/can

10 It

11 down

12 never/not

Vocabulary p14

Lead in

1 Ask students to read and understand the statements before they discuss them. If students are discussing the statements in groups, try to make sure the groups contain members of each sex in order to increase the level of discussion.

2 Encourage students to justify their choices. For example, ask *Why do you think some men are lazy?* (because they don't do enough housework).

3 Key

adventurous – adventure

competitive – competition

confident – confidence

cooperative – cooperation

emotional – emotion

generous – generosity
independent – independence
lazy – laziness
materialistic – materialism
optimistic – optimism
possessive – possession
self-centred – self-centredness
sensitive – sensitivity
sincere – sincerity
sociable – sociability
stubborn – stubbornness

Confusing verbs: *lay/lie*

5 Key

a 3   b 1   c 2

After they have done the matching exercise, check students understand by asking the following questions:

Is lay, meaning 'put or place something in a certain position', regular or irregular? (irregular) *What is the past form?* (laid) *What is the past participle?* (laid)

Is lie, meaning 'be in a flat resting position', regular or irregular? (irregular) *What is the past form?* (lay) *What is the past participle?* (lain)

Is lie, meaning the opposite of telling the truth, regular or irregular? (regular)

6 Key

a lie   d lay
b laid   e lied
c lying   f lay

7 Encourage students to give detailed answers.

Possible answers

a I always lie on my side, because I find it the most comfortable. If I lie on my back, I snore.

b My friend had her hair cut and I thought it looked terrible. She asked me if I liked it and I said yes. I lied because I didn't want to hurt her feelings.

Exam techniques p15
Listening Part 3

Dos and Don'ts

The exercise that follows introduces the type of multiple-matching exercise which appears in the exam. This section presents some useful strategies for dealing with it. Ask students to read the *Dos and Don'ts*. Check they understand by asking these questions: *What should you do first?* (read the instructions and options carefully) *How many options are not needed?* (one) *What should you listen for the first time you hear the recording?* (general understanding) *What should you make a note of?* (key words) *What else should you do?* (make a first choice of answers) *What should you listen for the second time you hear the recording?* (words associated with the options) *What do you do then?* (make a final choice of answer) *What do you do if you're not sure about an answer?* (write something – don't leave any spaces)

1 Key

Speaker 1   E
Speaker 2   D
Speaker 3   A
Speaker 4   F
Speaker 5   C

Audioscript

Speaker 1 I'd say that men and women are as good as each other at looking after children and loving them. I grew up without my dad around. At the time it seemed normal, but now I have my own kids I realise how mothers and fathers help us in different ways. As a dad myself, I know there's a bond between children and their dads that's just as important as having a mum around, and from experience **I'd say that only a man can really do that job.**

Speaker 2 If you're thinking about the day-to-day care of children, I'd say that fathers and mothers can be equally successful. I know several families where the mother is the main breadwinner and the father looks after the kids – and it works perfectly well. **But I'm sure that the physical relation between a baby and its mother creates an emotional tie which there's no substitute for,** and of course this won't change because men will never be able to have children.

Speaker 3 Mothers and fathers are different and always will be, but **both are essential. It's far too much work for one person to**

look after a family on their own, so it's important for the father to help out right from the start. The key thing is to always put the interests of the children first. I know that I have a special relationship with them as a mum, but I can see that my kids need their dad around too.

Speaker 4 The idea that men are worse at looking after children is rubbish. Dads can do everything just as well as mums. Women are only better at childcare because, at the moment, **they spend more time with kids than men do.** It's like my mum – she doesn't understand how to use email, but **if she worked in an office like me she'd know exactly what to do – it's just a question of familiarity.**

Speaker 5 When I was a kid, **my father made more effort to spend time with us than most fathers would have done, which wasn't what real men were supposed to do.** Whenever he wasn't at work, he dedicated all his time to me and my sisters. Other than my mum, people didn't really recognise how special he was. My father wasn't like everyone else, so people just ignored him. Nowadays, most men are involved with their kids like he was.

Phrasal verbs with *bring*

2 Key

a Bringing up
b bring (her) round
c brought about
d bring up
e brought out
f brought back
g bring down

Vocabulary p16

Formal and informal language

1 Possible answers

a Emails are replacing letters because they are easy to write, almost free to send, and because replies can be sent very quickly. Also, more and more people are using computers.

b People write emails more quickly and they take less care to avoid mistakes. People also approach emails more informally.

2 Key

a The first text is an email. The second is a formal letter.
b Both are intended as apologies.
c In the email, the reader and the writer are boyfriend and girlfriend. In the letter, they are probably business acquaintances.
d The email contains informal language, familiar situations, and contractions. The letter contains formal language, polite salutations, and full forms rather than contracted forms.
e The second text doesn't use contractions. Also, the fixed formal language is longer. Formal letters tend to use full sentences.

3 Key

a a snack
b attempted
c therefore
d sent you a text message
e to inform you
f because
g returned home
h I do apologise

4 Key

The email: was held up, didn't get in
The formal letter: was delayed, did not arrive

5 Key

a back down
b split up, went on
c put up with
d put me down
e bumped into
f called off
g brought up
h work out

Meanings of *get*

6 Key

get in – arrive home
got changed – changed
get you – contact you
get it – receive
got to – arrived at

Exam techniques p17
Use of English Part 4

Dos and Don'ts

The exercise that follows introduces the type of key word transformation exercise which appears in the exam. This section presents some useful strategies for dealing with it. Ask students to read the *Dos and Don'ts*. Check they understand by asking different students the following questions: *What should you do first for each sentence?* (read the first sentence and the gapped sentence) *What types of changes do you need to make?* (you may need to make the sentence passive, change the form of words, or add new words) *Can you change the key word?* (no) *How many words do you have to write?* (between two and five).

1 Key

1 get used to
2 have just been informed
3 three years since I saw
4 paid as much as men
5 have given up
6 reports of serious flooding
7 was advised to go
8 such an interesting book

Listening p18

Lead in

1 Ask students to justify their categorisation or give examples.

Possible answer

a Traditionally men have been thought to be better at subjects like Science and Mathematics. Women have been thought to be better at Art and Design and Foreign Languages. These days, these tendencies are less common. Women increasingly have better academic results in all subjects, especially at school.

b Traditionally, activities like Electrical repairs and Map-reading are associated with men, whereas woman are associated with Looking after children and Cooking. However, as with academic subjects, these ideas may not be true these days.

2 Key

a multitasking
b No, because people, especially women, may be expected to do more activities at the same time.

Audioscript

Presenter   In today's edition of *Focus on Gender* we focus on another of the supposed differences between men and women. I'll let our contributor Maggie Weston explain.

Maggie Weston   Hi, Sue, thanks. You know, it's several decades ago that women first challenged men's superiority in society, yet, as we all know, the old male/female stereotypes haven't gone away. People still believe, for example, that men are better at finding their way somewhere and that women are better at dealing with people, but in recent years a new difference between men and women has been discovered. I'm talking about multitasking – the ability to do several different things simultaneously, an apparently natural ability that most women have, but that most men can't comprehend. **Of course, this isn't actually a 'new' difference. Women have always had this ability** – it's simply that, until recently, men have been unaware of just how poor they are at multitasking themselves. Now, many men openly admit that women are superior in this area, and **admire them for being** able to multitask so efficiently. I recently overheard a 30-something-year-old man at a party saying – even boasting – that his wife could prepare dinner, talk to a friend on the phone, help their two children with their homework, and welcome him home from work all at the same time. The person he was telling came up with a similar story: his wife could read a book, watch television, and hold a conversation at the same time without a sign of panic. **For their part, most women take this ability for granted and can't understand why men find it so difficult.** They believe it's something they have had to learn in the modern world: society expects women to do everything, so that's what they have to do. Some even see it as a curse rather than a talent. A friend of mine said recently she thought that employers preferred to take on women because, unlike men, they could be relied on to do three things at the same time. The question that people are now asking is this: is the ability to multitask a genetic difference between the sexes, or is it something that women learn how to do from experience? According to neuroscientists, there are observable genetic differences between men's and women's brains, but these do not explain women's superiority when it comes to multitasking. **In fact, studies by scientists show that on average men and women are equally good at doing several tasks simultaneously.** A possible explanation for the apparent difference is that while men are capable of multitasking at work, they prefer to focus on one thing at a time in their home environment. **Women on the other hand are under more pressure at home to multitask, partly because men don't, or won't.** So there we have it. What do you think? I'll end with a quote from another friend of mine. I wonder if you'll agree with her when she said, and I quote: 'Who else has the time not to multitask except men?' Thanks for listening, even if you've been cooking lunch, writing another chapter of your latest novel, and planning your next holiday at the same time.

Multiple choice

3 Key

1 B	3 B	5 A
2 A	4 C	

Over to you

If students are working in groups, try to make sure there is a balance of the sexes in each group in order to increase discussion. Ask students to justify their opinions with reasons and examples. If necessary you can encourage further discussion by writing the following statements on the board and asking students to discuss them:

Women are good at looking after children because that is their natural function.

Women are not necessarily good at child-rearing. It is simply their traditional role.

Speaking p19

Lead in

2 Make sure students understand form-filling. Point out that it isn't necessary to write sentences, they can write one- or two-word answers. For example, write *Female* NOT *I'm female*.

3 Possible answers

How many brothers and sisters have you got?
Where do you live?
What kind of music do you like?
What do you do in your spare time?

Giving personal information

4 In Part 1 of the Speaking exam, students answer questions about their personal lives. These questions appear in the audioscript.

Key

Topics	Questions
Family	Do you have a large or a small family? Can you tell me something about them?
House and home	Do you live in a house or an apartment? What's it like? Could you tell us something about the area where you live?
Leisure	What do you like doing in your spare time? Do you have any hobbies? What kinds of books do you like to read? Do you play a musical instrument?

Audioscript

Interlocutor	My name's Petrina Cliff and this is my colleague Thorkild Gantner. He is just going to listen to us. So, you are?
Sun	Sun. My name is Sun.
Interlocutor	And?
Yasko	I'm Yasko. Yasko.
Interlocutor	Yasko?
Yasko	Yes.
Interlocutor	Thank you. First of all, we'd like to know something about you, so I'm going to ask you some questions about yourselves. Where are you from, Sun?
Sun	I'm from South Korea.
Interlocutor	And you, Yasko?
Yasko	I'm from Japan.
Interlocutor	Yasko, **do you have a large or a small family**?
Yasko	Err ... small family.
Interlocutor	**Can you tell me something about them?**
Yasko	Yes, I have two older brothers and I live with my father and mother. But two of my brothers have left er ... our home because they had got married before.
Interlocutor	**Do you live in a house or an apartment, Sun?**
Sun	**I live in my flat ... when I'm in Korea or London, which one?**
Interlocutor	In Korea.
Sun	In Korea then. I had own my flat in Korea then, and I used to stay there.
Interlocutor	**What's it like?**
Sun	Of course I like own my flat in ... which is located in Korea because the room is like studio. It's large and big and I had big, king-sized bed and then I used to live alone. But also, there is some kitchen and shower room with everything, so I like it. I'm still missing my room ... but ... Here is my flat is so small, but it's cosy.
Interlocutor	**Can you tell us something about the area where you live?**
Sun	In England?
Interlocutor	In Korea.
Sun	Erm ... because I stayed in the near the college, because I have to go to early in the college, but the place is quite nice, for example it's like national ... national park. Cos it's near the mountains and everything is good.

Interlocutor	Yasko, **what do you like doing in your spare time**?
Yasko	I like watching movies and ballet and listening to music.
Interlocutor	**And do you have any hobbies?**
Yasko	Yes, I like travelling.
Interlocutor	**What kind of books do you read?**
Sun	Erm ... now I don't read any book. But when I was in Korea I liked reading, especially like erm ... the thriller movie and thriller books and erm ... suspected, suspected books and I like, how do you say, I like Sherlock Holmes, that kind of book that I like.
Interlocutor	**Do you play a musical instrument, Yasko?**
Yasko	Yes, I ... I like playing the piano, but I'm not good at playing. But I enjoy .... enjoy playing the piano.
Interlocutor	How did you become interested in playing the piano?
Yasko	Pardon?
Interlocutor	**How did you become interested in playing the piano?**
Yasko	Yes. When I was small child my mother asked me to have a lesson, so at first I don't like to play the piano. But ... well ... when I was high-school student my friends said your play is very good so I have some confidence, so I become to like it.

6 Key

Extract 1: Yasko doesn't live with her brothers because they have got married.

Extract 2: Sun likes where he lives because it's part of a national park.

Extract 3: Sun enjoys thrillers.

Extract 4: Yasko became interested in playing the piano because her friends said she played well.

Audioscript

Extract 1

Interlocutor	Yasko, do you have a large or a small family?
Yasko	Err... small family.
Interlocutor	Can you tell me something about them?
Yasko	Yes, I have two older brothers and I live with my father and mother. **But two of my brothers have left er ... our home because they had got married before.**

Extract 2

Interlocutor	Could you tell us something about the area where you live?
Sun	In England?
Interlocutor	In Korea.
Sun	Erm ... because I stayed in the near the college, because I have to go to early in the college, but **the place is quite nice, for example it's like national ... national park. Cos it's near the mountains and everything is good.**

Extract 3

Interlocutor	What kinds of books do you like to read?
Sun	Erm ... now I don't read any book. But when I was in Korea **I liked reading, especially like erm ... the thriller movie and thriller books and erm ...** suspected, suspected books and I like, how do you say, I like Sherlock Holmes, that kind of book that I like.

Extract 4

Interlocutor	How did you become interested in playing the piano?
Yasko	Pardon?
Interlocutor	How did you become interested in playing the piano?
Yasko	Yes. When I was small child my mother asked me to have a lesson, so at first I don't like to play the piano. But ... well **... when I was high-school student my friends said your play is very good so I have some confidence, so I become to like it.**

7 Ask students to read the tip box. Check understanding by asking the following questions: *What kind of answers should you give to questions during the speaking exam?* (full answers) *What shouldn't you do?* (answer with a few words or single sentences)

Whilst students are doing the task, monitor their discussions and give feedback to the class about their performance at the end. (Did they avoid answering with just a few words? Did they give full answers?)

Writing p20

Informal letter or email

1 The exercise which follows introduces emails as a transactional writing task for FCE Writing Part 1. Tell students that the task can require either a letter or an email, and that the style can be formal or informal. Each task can include any of the following functions: giving or requesting information, making complaints, corrections or suggestions. Tell them they should be sure that they have read and understood all the information they are given before they begin the task.

Key

a The email must give information about the weather and accommodation. It must also include suggestions about activities to do.
b The email should be informal. Sam is a friend of yours.

2 Key

The reply includes the relevant information, but the style is too formal in places. The writer uses some very polite phrases (*In response to your question, As for*).

3 Key

a	INF	e	F
b	F	f	INF
c	INF	g	INF
d	F	h	INF

4 Key

a Short sentences – *Fantastic news!*
c Contractions – *I'd forgotten, It's difficult, There'll be*
f Phrasal verbs – *We must meet up*
g Words left out – *Hope your exams go well* (missing *I*)
h Simple words or slang – *pretty warm, loads of things*

Think, plan, write

5 After they have read the task and decided on the style, ask the following questions to check understanding: *Who has sent you a letter?* (an English-speaking friend, Jo) *What is he/she planning to do?* (spend a year in your country, learn the language, and work) *What advice does he/she need?* (where to work, where to study, and where to live).

Key

informal

Overview p22

1 Key

  1 A
  2 A
  3 B
  4 C
  5 C
  6 C
  7 A
  8 B

2 Key

a brought up	d bring about
b brings back	e brought up
c bring round	

3 Key

a understand	d took/caught; arrived
b make/buy	e becoming
c buy	

An extra activity to accompany this unit and a unit test can be downloaded from the Internet at www.oup.com/elt/teacher/exams

2 Compulsion

Introduction p23

1 If students find this difficult, make sure they recognise the central action of each photo. (Photo 1, using a games console; Photo 2, sending text messages; Photo 3, smoking; Photo 4, eating junk food and using audio devices; Photo 5, gambling; Photo 6, shopping).

Possible answer

a The unit title *Compulsion* refers to activities that people can't stop doing. The pictures show activities which people often get addicted to.

2 Possible answers

a Some people seem to become more easily addicted than others. This might be due to personality traits, but social conditions may also be a factor.

b People's lives can be affected if addictions prevent them from getting on with everyday activities. Addictions may affect people's finances, cause ill-health, or lead to the breakdown of relationships.

c Education can play a big part in helping people avoid addiction. If education fails, banning people from certain activities can stop people becoming addicted.

Listening p24

Lead in

3 Key

a teenagers and digital technology

b three distinguished experts: a child psychologist, a headteacher, and a university counsellor.

4 Key

a texting his friends at mealtimes

b a temporary addiction / a phase

Audioscript

Presenter	In this evening's *Phone the experts* we're starting off with a subject which has clearly got a good many of you out there worried. We'll be discussing the subject of teenagers and digital technology. It appears that this is not just an issue that worries parents, but something that increasingly concerns young people themselves. On our studio panel we have three distinguished experts: Evan Matthews, a child psychologist, Joanne Carter, a secondary school headteacher, and Liz Polanski, who has three teenagers of her own and is a university counsellor who helps students with their problems. Our first caller this evening is James Benson. Hi James, how are you doing?
James	Hi. I'm fine.
Presenter	What's your question for our panel?

Sentence completion

5 Key

a digital friends

b two and five

c text messages

d adults

e dad

f less time

Audioscript

Presenter	What's your question for our panel?
James	I'd like to know what you think about my parents' behaviour over the last few weeks.
Presenter	Your parents?
James	That's right. **They're getting more and more obsessed about the amount of time I spend with what they call my 'digital friends'.**

Evan	Hi James. Can you tell me who exactly these friends are?
James	Just people I've met on the Internet.
Evan	And what contact do you have with them in a normal day?
James	Well, when I wake up in the morning, I always turn on my computer to see if anyone's sent me any emails or put a comment on *MySpace* for me. Then I usually check my mobile to see if anyone's left me a message.
Evan	How long does all that usually take?
James	**About five minutes if I have to reply to any messages or emails. If I don't, it only takes me about two minutes.**
Joanne	Five minutes every morning doesn't sound too bad to me. What about later in the day?
James	It depends if I'm at college or at home. If I don't have to go to college, I usually go on MSN for a couple of hours in the morning, and maybe a couple more in the evening.
Joanne	Hmm, four hours a day – that does sound rather a lot.
James	I suppose so, but **what Mum and Dad really object to me doing is texting my friends at mealtimes.** They're always accusing me of being rude and anti-social.
Joanne	And what do you think?
James	I just think it's normal behaviour for people of my age.
Joanne	How many texts do you send a day?
James	I don't normally keep count, but probably about thirty or forty.
Joanne	OK – and do you understand why your parents are getting so annoyed?
James	Not really. It's just a bit of fun. **I think adults tend to be too serious about things**. I bet when they were young they used to do things that annoyed their parents.
Liz	Can I ask you, James, do you have any other interests outside your digital world? I mean do you play any sports?
James	Not now. **I used to go swimming regularly and play tennis with my dad.**
Liz	But not any longer?
James	No, my dad's always too busy. I remember last summer every time I suggested a game of tennis, he'd say he was too busy. Now it's the opposite problem – it's me that's too busy.
Presenter	OK James, I think we get an idea of what your life is like. I'd like to invite each of our experts to comment on what they've heard. Can I start with you, Evan?
Evan	OK James. You phoned the programme to complain about your parents' attitude towards you. Having heard you talk about your life, I have to say I completely understand and sympathise with your parents and what you're putting them through. They feel like they're losing you to your digital friends. **I suggest you spend less time on MSN and on your mobile** and make sure you spend at least a couple of hours a day on other things – preferably interacting with real people – including your parents.
Presenter	Thanks, Evan. OK – would you like to go next Joanne?
Joanne	Sure. OK James, here's what I suggest. I think you should realise that you have a addiction – not very different from the way people become drug or alcohol addicts. Obviously you can't stop altogether – the shock to your system would be too great, but what I suggest you do is try to cut back by a few minutes every day, so that by this time next year your life is back in some kind of balance. Get back to going swimming and playing tennis with your dad – and of course spend time hanging out with your real friends! I'm sure you'll be happier that way. You won't lose any genuine friends and you won't have your parents on your back all the time.
Presenter	OK and lastly, Liz.
Liz	Right, James. If my own teenage son's experience is anything to go by, I think your addiction is probably a very temporary one. I guess in another month or two you'll find you get bored with your digital life – and almost without thinking about it, you'll slip back into the kind of life you had before you caught this digital virus. In other words I'd say you're going through a phase.
Presenter	Thank you all very much – and thank you James for your very intriguing question. I suppose we haven't really answered the question you asked, but I think all three of our experts have come up with ideas that should improve your family situation overall.
James	Thanks very much.

6 Key

anti-social, impolite, rude
assertive, determined, stubborn
depressed, fed up, unhappy
exhausted, overtired, sleepy

Grammar and practice p25

Habits

1 Key

a, b, c, d, f

Verb forms in the present simple and the verb *tend to* are used to indicate the present, plus use of frequency adverbs (*always, sometimes, usually*).

2 Key

e, g

Verbs forms *would* and *used to* and the past simple are used to indicate the past, plus use of time references like *Last summer*.

3 Possible answers

never
rarely
hardly ever
occasionally
frequently
often

After students have complete the task, encourage them to refer to the Grammar reference on page 175.

4 Possible answers

a When people are *fed up*, they tend to be miserable, unsociable and unwilling to go out and do things.

b When people are *nervous* or *embarrassed*, they tend to blush and be unable to speak clearly. Sometimes they become clumsy.

c When people are *excited*, they tend to talk and laugh a lot. They tend to rush about and do a lot of things.

5 Key

The present continuous with *always* is used to refer to very frequent actions, especially ones which the speaker finds annoying.

Used to

7 After students have completed the task, encourage them to refer to the Grammar reference on page 175.

Key

a 3 b 1 c 2

8 Key

a 'll never get used to d aren't used to
b aren't used to e 'm used to
c get used to

Cloze

10 Key

1 the
2 their
3 where
4 or
5 to
6 that
7 much
8 with
9 but
10 who/that
11 from
12 on

Vocabulary p27

Lead in

Check students understand the meaning of the title: *confessions* (something wrong that people admit to doing), *chocoholic* (somebody who is obsessed with eating chocolate).

1 Key

The writer feels a bit *defensive* that the reader might laugh at him/her, *proud* that he/she has got the addiction under control at the moment, and also a bit *smug* that he/she doesn't put on any weight even when he/she eats a lot of chocolate.

Phrasal verbs

3 Key

cut down – reduced
get by – survive
light up – shine
turns off – disgusts
putting on – gaining
give up – stop

4 Key

a 4, 6 c 1, 7 e 3
b 5 d 2

5 Key

a give (it) back d give in
b giving up on e giving out
c giving away

Exam techniques p28

Reading Part 3

Dos and Don'ts

The exercise that follows introduces the type of multiple-matching exercise which appears in the exam. This section presents some useful strategies for dealing with it. Ask students to read the *Dos and Don'ts*. Check they understand by asking these questions: *What should you do when you first read the text?* (find out what information you're looking for) *What should you do the second time?* (read for general understanding; make a note of any answers) *What should you look for in the questions?* (key words) *What parts of the text should you reread?* (only those relevant to the questions) *What should you do if you can't find the information immediately?* (go on to the next question) *What should you do if you're not sure about an answer?* (make a sensible guess)

1 Before students begin the task, you may like to check that they understand the meaning of these words: *passive smoking* (breathing in other people's smoke), *wheezy* (having difficulty with breathing), *wasted* (weak, not as strong as they used to be), *lungs* (part of body required for breathing), *resistance* (ability to fight against something), *gesticulate* (use your hands to give a message), *subjected* (forced to put up with), *self-conscious* (embarrassed), *introverted* (shy, withdrawn), *hostile* (unfriendly), *quit* (given up), *lousy* (terrible).

Key

1, 2	D/E	7	H
3	A	8, 9, 10	A/F/H
4	G	11, 12	B/G
5	C	13, 14	F/H
6	F	15	A

Over to you

If relevant to your class, pair smokers with non-smokers to increase the level of discussion. Encourage students to give reasons for their opinions.

Vocabulary p30

Lead in

Before students read the article, check they understand the meaning of *superstition* (irrational belief based on omens, good luck charms, etc.).

Check students understand the meaning of the extract by asking these questions: *What two superstitions does the narrator's sister have?* (She won't walk under ladders, and she won't open an umbrella inside the house.) *What about the narrator's brother?* (He touches wood for luck.) *How does the narrator feel about people who are superstitious?* (It's understandable because it's a natural human characteristic.)

Comparison

3 Key

worse, the least superstitious, as superstitious as, most natural, more mystical

4 After students have completed the task, encourage them to refer to the Grammar reference on page 176.

Key

a longer, longest; shorter, shortest
b larger, largest; later, latest
c flatter, flattest; thinner, thinnest
d heavier, heaviest; funnier, funniest
e more important, most important; more independent, most independent
f cleverer/more clever, cleverest/most clever; narrower/more narrow, narrowest/most narrow
g better, best; worse, worst
h more easily, most easily; more carefully, most carefully

5 Key

very different: far, a lot, much
almost the same: a bit, a little, slightly

6 Key

a the unluckiest
b more dangerous
c hotter
d the worst, more neatly
e younger/youngest, cleverer/more clever
f the shortest, the most intelligent

Speaking p31

Lead in

In the first part of the Speaking exam, the students are asked personal questions such as these about themselves, their families and their interests. In this case, they can do the activity in pairs.

Long turn

This task represents Part 2 of the exam. Students can work in pairs. Before they begin, ask them to read the information in the tip box at the bottom of the page. Check understanding by asking these questions: *How many photos is each student asked to talk about in the exam?* (two) *What should you do when you're talking about them?* (say what is similar and what is different) *What shouldn't you do?* (describe each picture separately)

Draw attention to the kind of comparing and contrasting expressions they should be using. Ask for more suggestions of suitable language:

This photo shows … but this photo …

In both photos you can see …

These people look much …. than …

Whilst students are doing the task, monitor their discussions and give feedback to the class about their performance. (Did they talk about both photos? Did they compare the two photos effectively? Did they use the language of comparison effectively?)

3 Possible answer

Photos 1 and 2 show groups of people at different types of gathering: one group are sports fans and the others are motorbike riders. While the activities are quite different, members of each group have a kind of uniform that they use to express their identity. People like these often behave and dress the same way so that they can feel part of the same group and easily identify each other.

4 Possible answer

Photos 3 and 4 show people doing activities on their own. Photo 3 shows a young woman walking in a wilderness area, while photo 4 shows an older woman painting a picture. Both are quiet activities, but the first is more energetic. People who like to concentrate on an activity without needing to cooperate with others will prefer doing activities on their own.

Writing p32

Article

1 Possible answers

1 on the train/bus, in the bath, when they are relaxing, in doctors' or dentists' waiting rooms.

2 It may depend on whether they are interested in the subject, whether the writing style is accessible, or how well the article is presented on the page.

3 Informal – the article is intended for young people, it is about a light-hearted subject and the title *I'm just crazy about …* is an informal expression.

2 Key

a by talking about it from a personal viewpoint

c informal, personal, serious

d paragraph 3

e a lot of extreme adjectives, e.g. fantastic, terrifying

Creating interest

3 Key

It should attract your attention.
It should make you want to read the article.
It should give you an idea of what the text is about.

4 Possible answers

The title *No, I'm not completely mad* is the most likely to make somebody want to read on because it creates an element of mystery. It gives no idea what the article is going to be about but suggests that it is something unusual. Readers may be curious to find out what that is.

Sky-diving for beginners – This title is fairly bland, although it might attract somebody who wants to learn about sky-diving.

So you'd like to try sky-diving – This title is also fairly bland, although it is intended as a question directed at the reader, which might attract attention.

A complete history of sky-diving – This title suggests something that is serious, dense and possibly dull.

5 Possible answers

Have you ever wondered what it would be like to fall out of an aeroplane? This sentence immediately engages the reader by asking a dramatic question.

The other sentences in comparison are not so
interesting.

Think, plan, write

6 After students have read the task, ask them these
questions to check they understand what they
have to do. *Where will the article be published?* (in
an English-language magazine) *Who will read it?*
(students of a similar age) *What is the title of the
article?* (I've always wanted to …) *What is the
subject?* (an activity you'd like to try) *How long
should the article be?* (120–180 words)

8 Before students make their notes, encourage
them to refer to the Writing guide on page 166.

Overview p34

1 Key

1 from	7 after
2 of	8 with
3 in	9 out
4 does	10 to
5 Not	11 when / if / whenever
6 because	12 later / after

2 Key

a 2	c 4	e 3
b 5	d 1	

3 Key

a determined	d stubborn
b sleepy	e rude
c fed up	f assertive

An extra activity to accompany this unit and a unit
test can be downloaded from the Internet at
www.oup.com/elt/teacher/exams

3 Talents

Introduction p35

1 Possible answers

  a Photo 1: This person is a gymnast. To do this, you must have physical strength and a high level of coordination.

     Photo 2: This person is fishing. Fishing requires a good knowledge of the environment. You also need to have a lot of patience to do this well.

     Photo 3: This person is a model. To do this, you normally have to be tall, thin, good-looking and confident, which are qualities you are born with. However, you also need to learn how to walk on the catwalk.

     Photo 4: This person is a surgeon. To do this, you need concentration and intelligence, but you also needs years of education and training so that you can do your job competently and with confidence.

     Photo 5: These people are actors. To do this well, you require some natural talent, but it is possible to improve your skills at drama school. Good looks and a clear voice can help in this job.

  c In business, ambition can help you do well. Business people often need to be persuasive. To be successful, it helps to have some money in the first place so that you can invest.
In the film and music industries, it is increasingly important to be good-looking. Getting started in these industries is difficult, but having good connections can help.

Reading p36

Gapped text

3 You may like to check that students understand the meaning of these words: *scholarship* (money paid by an organisation to help pay for someone's education), *acclaimed* (praised by lots of people), *intensive* (involving a lot of activity in a short time), *an adrenaline junkie* (somebody addicted to exciting activities), *gritty* (showing things as they really are), *cemented* (fixed firmly), *dashing* (attractive, confident and elegant).

As they do the task, encourage students to underline parts of the paragraphs that help them decide on the correct answers.

Key

1 C	4 H	6 F
2 G	5 B	7 E
3 A		

Option D is not needed.

Phrasal verbs with *turn*

4 Key

a 3	d 2	f 4
b 7	e 1	g 6
c 5		

Grammar and practice p38

Can, be able to

1 Key

a Orlando Bloom *is able to* ride a horse bareback while shooting an arrow.

b He *couldn't* swordfight before the filming of *The Lord of the Rings*.

2 Key

a There is no infinitive form of *can*.

b There is no past participle form of *can*. Consequently, there is no present perfect or past perfect form of *can*.

3 Key

a He can run 100 metres in just over twelve seconds.

b When I was younger, I could climb a mountain without getting out of breath.

c They had eaten such a big breakfast that they couldn't finish their lunch.

d He could probably touch his toes if he lost weight.

e Even if I'd been stronger, I couldn't have lifted those heavy weights.

4 Key

Could cannot be used to talk about an ability to do something on a particular occasion. *Could* is used to talk about more general abilities.

Encourage students to refer to the Grammar reference on page 178.

Other ability structures

5 Encourage students to refer to the Grammar reference on page 178.

Key

It's talking about a general ability in the past, not about a particular occasion.

6 Key

b didn't succeed in finding

c wasn't able to finish

d succeeded in passing

e managed to break in

f was(n't) able to swim

g managed/has managed to get

h wasn't able to fall

i succeeded in opening

j Have (you) managed to lose

7 Key

b, c, f, h

8 Ask students to read the text quickly before they begin the task. Check they understand the meaning of these words and phrases: *dextrous* (clever/skilled with your hands), *run before they can walk* (do things too quickly, not take the time to learn the basics of something), *session* (period of time training).

Check students understand the writer's attitude by asking: *Does the writer consider that only naturally talented people can be successful jugglers?* (No. The writer thinks anybody can train themselves.) *What qualities does the writer think are essential?* (patience and the determination to practise) *How long does the writer think it takes to become a performing juggler?* (not very long – three half-hour sessions followed by a further hour and a half of practice).

Key

1 to learn how to

2 is able to throw/can throw

3 to be good at

4 can't/won't be able to

5 manage to catch

Cloze

10 Check students understand the meaning of these words and phrases: *emigrated* (moved to live permanently in another country), *trapeze* (a bar hanging from two pieces of rope in the circus), *handcuffs* (metal rings joined by a chain used for holding prisoners' hands together), *straitjacket* (a jacket with long arms which are tied to prevent the person wearing it becoming violent), *suspended* (hanging from something else), *regurgitate* (to bring swallowed food back up), *dislocate* (put a bone out of its normal position in a joint), *ruptured* (broken or burst apart).

Key

1 when	7 could
2 as	8 able
3 on	9 is/was
4 could/would	10 being/and
5 of	11 did
6 over	12 most

Vocabulary p40

Lead in

1 Possible answers

jumping from high buildings, taking part in car chases, riding motorbikes, parachuting from aeroplanes, fighting, jumping on and off horses

2 Key

They least like to fall under a moving train.

Film vocabulary

3 Possible answers

a actors/actresses, directors, producers, scriptwriters, lighting engineers, costume designers, casting directors, etc.

b thriller, horror film, love story, war film, historical drama, documentary, etc.

4 Key

a	subtitles	f	ending
b	acting	g	Animated
c	plot	h	cast
d	soundtrack	i	script
e	special effects	j	stars

Exam techniques p41

Listening Part 1

Dos and Don'ts

The exercise that follows introduces the type of multiple-choice exercise which appears in the exam. This section presents some useful strategies for dealing with it. Ask students to read the *Dos and Don'ts*. Check they understand by asking these questions: *What should you do first?* (read and listen to the first question and the options carefully) *What should you do the first time you listen?* (mark the options you think are possible) *What should you do the second time?* (check your ideas and make your final choice) *What should you do for the next questions?* (follow the same procedure) *What is it important to concentrate on?* (the extract you are about to hear, not the last one)

1 Key

1 C	4 A	7 C
2 A	5 B	8 A
3 C	6 C	

Audioscript

1

Woman Yes, he is one of the big box-office draws. They make millions of dollars out of his films so he's obviously popular. **I think it's more to do with the image he puts across than anything else. He always plays the part of a hard, tough macho guy, and I suppose he appeals to young people, particularly boys and young men, for that reason.** I mean, well he's quite nice to look at if you like men with muscles – which not everyone does of course. But you wouldn't exactly call him a brilliant actor, would you? So I suppose it must be that.

2

Woman I don't see what the problem is. Can't you just say you're a friend of the director's? I mean you are anyway.

Man That won't make any difference. It doesn't really have anything to do with him.

Woman Well, don't you know 'thingy', 'what's his name', the main actor?

Man Steve Andrew? Yes, but I can hardly bother him with this, can I?

Woman Well, can't you do something? I'd be ideal. I'm tall and blonde. You said that was what they were looking for? **It's not as if I need loads of experience to be an extra, is it?**

3

Man I wouldn't say it was his best film. But it was a lot better than his last one, that's for sure. That was far too long. They could have cut it by at least thirty minutes. But, in this film, **the bit where he arranges to meet the girl and there's this incredible mix up was well done. And the scene with his father at the end.** Yeah, it was a pleasant way to spend an afternoon.

4

Man No, I know you can't give me my money back … that's not why I'm ringing. **I just want to know if it's possible to come another day instead** … Yes, I understand that, but surely you can sell these tickets and give me some others? … No, that doesn't matter … That would be fine, actually. The seats aren't too near the front, are they? … Row M. No, that'll be fine. Well, thanks a lot. **That's great. I'll pick them up tomorrow.**

5

Woman I don't think making it into a conference hall is a bad idea exactly. I'm not against it. I just think it would be too expensive. I rather like John's idea of dividing it up into four or five smaller cinemas and I think we should seriously consider lowering the original ceiling. We'd save a lot on heating costs and it should improve the sound quality as well. **Obviously we'd have to replace all the old seats too.**

6

Man   What? Oh, for goodness sake! I don't believe it! You can't do anything right, can you? **I distinctly said not the back row.** You know your mother can't see a thing unless she's practically sitting on top of the screen. Well, you'll just have to phone up the box-office and get it sorted out, won't you? 'Cos I'm not. And I'm not paying for those seats either.

7

Man 1   Who chose Branson for the part anyway?

Man 2   Me, I'm afraid. The agency didn't have anyone else even remotely suitable. I knew he wouldn't be brilliant but I didn't think he'd be this bad I have to admit.

Man 1   Well, it's too late to do anything about it now. We're already behind schedule. **We'll just have to do without that scene.** Let the scriptwriter know, will you? In case he needs to make any changes.

8

Woman   **It was an all–girls' secondary school and it was very much geared towards preparing pupils for university.** So when Mary said she wanted to go to drama school to study acting instead of taking up her university place, the headmistress wasn't at all pleased. We were all quite envious of her. It sounded much more glamorous than anything we were going to do. And of course the headmistress was proved wrong when Mary went on to be a huge success.

Over to you

Possible answer

Good actors may be born with certain qualities, but they can improve their skills at drama school. Part of their ability may be inherited since lots of famous actors and actresses have famous parents too.

Famous people, like actors, musicians, and politicians may follow their parents and have more opportunities in that field. This can also be true of other professions such as doctors and lawyers.

Vocabulary p42

Lead in

Background information

The photos show (left) Spanish racing driver Fernando Alonso and (right) Italian footballer Gianluca Zambrotta.

Noun suffixes

3 Possible answers

motor racing: aggressive, ambitious, brave, determined, fit
football: accurate, aggressive, ambitious, athletic, determined, fit

4 Key

accuracy	determination
aggression	fairness
ambition	fitness
arrogance	honesty
athleticism	intelligence
bravery	reliability

5 Key

adult (noun)	disagree (verb)
friend (noun)	justify (verb)
act (verb)	occur (verb)
teach (verb)	

6 Possible answers

-hood: childhood, neighbourhood
-ship: leadership, membership
-or: instructor, director
-er: player, driver
-ment: employment, amusement
-tion: invitation, introduction
-ence: reference, existence

7 Key

a Participation	d supporters
b Childhood	e obligation
c sponsorship	f performance

Exam techniques p43

Use of English Part 3

Dos and Don'ts

The exercise that follows introduces the type of word formation exercise which appears in the exam. This section presents some useful strategies for dealing with it. Ask students to read the *Dos and Don'ts*. Check they understand by asking these questions: *What should you do first?* (read the text quickly and get an idea of the topic) *What should you do the second time you read the text?* (try to decide what kind of word is missing) *What should you do to the word in capitals?* (change it into the kind of word you need) *What do you do when you have finished changing the words?* (read through the text) *What should you do if you're not sure about an answer?* (make a guess)

1 Key

B

2 Background information

The photo shows Maria Sharapova, one of the top tennis players in the world.

Key

1 earnings	6 hardly
2 successful	7 unable
3 income	8 famous
4 sponsorship	9 failure
5 millionaires	10 psychological

Over to you

Possible answers

Some people argue that women should receive the same prize money as male tennis players because they work as hard and the tickets to games are the same price. However, opponents argue that men play for longer (five sets) and at a higher level.

Listening p44

Sentence completion

2 Ask students to read the gapped sentences before they listen to the interview. Play the recording and students complete the gaps. play the recording a second time if necessary.

Key

1 the United States
2 dangers
3 (very) difficult / anything but easy
4 eat
5 the poorest families
6 time and money
7 free time

Audioscript

Presenter	This afternoon we have in the studio the leading American child psychiatrist Dr. Ambrose Taylor, author of the book *Raising the next Tiger Woods*. Pleased to have you join us, Dr. Taylor.
Dr Taylor	I'm very pleased to be here.
Presenter	Now your book, I believe, is out here next month.
Dr Taylor	I believe so, yes.
Presenter	**And it has aroused a lot of interest – and criticism too, I might add – in the United States.**
Dr Taylor	That's very true.
Presenter	Now, for the benefit of the listeners, I think we should point out that it's not actually about what to do if you want your child to be the next Tiger Woods, is it?
Dr Taylor	**No, it's more about the dangers of hyper-parenting.**
Presenter	And by 'hyper-parenting' you mean?
Dr Taylor	I mean treating your children as if they were in a competition. Hustling them from activity to activity in order to make their future resumé – or CV, for you – as impressive as possible.
Presenter	**Now, it seems to me that raising a child is anything but easy these days** and that parents can't win. It used to be the case that if you took an interest in your child's development you were seen as a 'good' parent. Now you're just as likely to be seen as a 'pushy' parent.
Dr Taylor	That is true. And it <u>is</u> very difficult for parents I agree. Unfortunately, what has happened is that parents have been led to believe that if they do all the right things, they can somehow programme their children for success. And it starts even before the children are born. **Pregnant mothers are told what they should and shouldn't eat**, and then after the baby's born they're told that if they play it Mozart this could speed its development, so they play it Mozart, and it just goes on from there.
Presenter	So are you saying that this advice is wrong?
Dr Taylor	I'm saying that advice like this has helped to create a very 'winner-takes-all' society – a sort of competition culture if you like.
Presenter	Now you are an American and you have written about the situation over there. Would you say that the same applied here?
Dr Taylor	Most definitely, yes. And in other parts of Europe too.

Presenter	And would you say that this affects all sections of society?
Dr Taylor	**I'd say it's pretty much the norm for all but the poorest families.**
Presenter	But this is just keeping up with the Joneses, isn't it? This is nothing new.
Dr Taylor	It isn't new, no. What is new though is the fact that, whereas before there were <u>some</u> parents who would push their children, this wasn't the norm. Now it is the norm. Parenting has become a very competitive thing. Parents are sending their children to gym classes or judo when they're five, French lessons when they're six. It has become a crazy sort of competition.
Presenter	I imagine that parents who do this think that they're doing the right thing by giving their children the opportunity to develop any talents they might have, aren't they?
Dr Taylor	Of course. They believe that if they don't push their children they are letting them down.
Presenter	So are you condemning this outright?
Dr Taylor	No, I am not condemning it outright. What I <u>am</u> saying is that there are dangers in it. If a child is very good at something, then of course a parent should support them and encourage them, but they need to be honest with themselves and ask themselves whether the interest is really the child's and not their own. **Also, a lot of problems can arise where parents invest an awful lot of their time and money in their children** and their children cannot live up to their expectations. It can be very destructive for the relationship and for the child's self-esteem. Not every child is going to grow up to be the next Tiger Woods or Venus Williams.
Presenter	So what is the answer?
Dr Taylor	The answer lies somewhere in the middle. Organise some structured activity for the child, by all means – if it's something that the child is genuinely interested in – but don't fill their day with structured activities. Give them some free time to fill for themselves. **Children need to learn to manage their free time**, otherwise when they get older and leave home they will lack the most basic self-management skills. They will simply not know what to do with their time.
Presenter	That does seem like basic common sense, yes.
Dr Taylor	And don't expect your child to be the next Tiger Woods either. It's only a few that will reach that level.
Presenter	No. Well thank you for coming on the programme today, Dr Taylor. It's been very interesting. Now some music ...

Confusing verbs: *rise, arise, raise*

3 Key

a problem arises
a situation arises
raise someone's hopes
raise money
unemployment rises
raise the alarm
the sun rises

4 Before students do this exercise, check that they know the past and past participle forms of the verbs.

raise   raised   raised (transitive)

rise   rose   risen (intransitive)

arise   arose   arisen (intransitive)

Key

a	raising	d	arises
b	arise	e	was raised
c	rose		

Speaking p45

Two-way task

2 This task represents Part 3 of the exam. Explain that in this part students will be given a sheet on which there are a number of related pictures. They should discuss these in order to complete a task. Before students begin, ask them to read the information in the tip box.

Monitor students as they do the task without interrupting, and give feedback to the class at the end. (Did they listen to each other properly? Did they keep the conversation going by making appropriate contributions? Did they discuss each job in terms of abilities and personal qualities? Did they complete the task by agreeing on the two jobs they would find most interesting?)

Possible answers

A *reporter* needs to be curious, determined, and clearly-spoken.

A *teacher* needs to be intelligent, assertive, and approachable, as well as having an ability to explain difficult things.

A *lifeguard* needs to be brave and physically fit, as well as being able to swim well and give first aid.
A *nurse* needs to be sympathetic, dedicated and capable of carrying out medical procedures.
A *travel agent* needs to be courteous and persuasive, and have a good knowledge of travel options.
A *DJ* needs to be charismatic and have a good knowledge of up-to-date music and how to use the turntables.

Discussion

Part 4 of the Speaking paper asks a number of questions that are related to the topic of Part 3. Students can continue to work in pairs for this task.

Writing p46

Letter of application

1 When students have read the advert, check understanding by asking the following questions: *What is the job for?* (tour guides) *What abilities do you need to have?* (speak English; be interested in the history of your town; be good at organising; be reliable) *What are the lengths of the contracts?* (one month, two months, three months) *Do you need experience/training?* (No, training is given.)

   Key
   b Dear Sir/Madam, Yours faithfully
   c The style will be formal.
   d You should include details of knowledge of local history, proof of organisational skills and reliability, also any qualifications, languages and relevant experience (although not a requirement).

2 **Key**
   b Yes, they have: she has studied English for five years; she is a reliable person; she has been responsible for organising sports and games; she is interested in the history of Palermo.

3 **Key**
   I would like to apply for …
   … as advertised in …
   I have just finished …
   I am looking for …
   I would be available to work for …
   With regard to your requirements, I believe I meet all of them.

I have been told that I am a … person
I was responsible for …
I look forward to hearing from you and wish to advise you that I am available for interview at any time.

4 **Key**
   Dear Sir or Madam**,**
   studying **E**nglish
   organising activities**. L**ast summer
   … said [']he would be happy to employ me again['].
   Palermo, I am interested
   Your[']s

5 **Key**
   b last year, but I had (*but* is used to join two sentences and is normally preceded by a comma when the second sentence has its own subject)
   c good. I can (These are two sentences which must be separated by a full stop)
   d an interview, I am available (*If*-clauses which come at the start of a sentence are followed by a comma)
   e Wednesday, when I attend (a comma must be used before a non-defining relative clause)
   f my school, although (clauses beginning with *although, despite,* and *in spite of* are preceded by a comma)
   g twenty-two-year-old (this phrase needs hyphens when it occurs before the noun)
   h University, so this (clauses beginning with *so* are normally part of the same sentence)
   i references? (questions always require a question mark)
   j referee[']s (plural nouns do not require an apostrophe before the 's')

Think, plan, write

6 When students have read the advert, check understanding by asking the following questions: *What is the job for?* (to help organise sports and other activities at American summer camps for children) *How old must you be?* (eighteen or over) *How long must you be available to work for?* (at least nine weeks) *When does the job start?* (June 15) *What abilities do you need to have?* (be fit, enthusiastic and responsible)

Overview p48

1 Key

1 Nearly	6 passionate
2 successful	7 essential
3 composer	8 refusal
4 extraordinary	9 reinvented
5 influential	10 resemblance

2 Key

a Could
b didn't manage
c succeeded
d haven't managed
e Can
f couldn't/weren't able to
g could
h succeeded

3 Key

a out	e into
b back	f up
c down	g over
d to	

An extra activity to accompany this unit and a unit test can be downloaded from the Internet at www.oup.com/elt/teacher/exams

4 Appearances

Introduction p49

2 When students have read the extract, ask them the following questions: *Which two words or phrases mean 'tricked'?* (taken in, conned) *What two examples of trickery are given?* (salespeople getting people to buy things; politicians getting people to vote for them)

Listening p50

Lead in

1 Before students do the tasks, ask them to identify what the people in the photos are probably doing or what they are about to do. (Left to right: going to work, going to school/college, playing sport, going out for a social occasion)

Multiple matching

2 Before students do the task, ask them to look back at the list of *Dos and Don'ts* on page 15 for ways of approaching a Part 3 Listening task.

Key

Speaker 1	D	Speaker 4	A
Speaker 2	F	Speaker 5	B
Speaker 3	C		

Audioscript

Speaker 1 **It's not what you'd call trendy, but at least you don't have to worry about what to put on in the mornings. Some of the rules are incredible, though. You just wouldn't believe them.** Listen to this one: 'Pupils must wear ties at all times.' Or this: 'Boys must not wear baseball caps in class.' There was a row here recently when they sent my mate home and told him to get his hair cut. And I think the rule about not letting boys wear earrings is very unfair. Some of the girls wear skirts which are much shorter than the regulation length. In the end, it's something else to rebel against, isn't it?

Speaker 2 It's a constant battle. So far I've flatly refused to pay more than £30 for trainers. But Adriano's desperate for a pair of the new Nikes, and the cheapest I've found is £50. He says he wants them because they're more comfortable than other makes, and apparently they're lighter and better designed than the ones he's got at the moment. **The truth is his friends at school have all got this sort, and they make fun of him because he hasn't.** He's just so persistent. I'll probably give in eventually.

Speaker 3 **I've always based my creations on what's happening out there on the streets. Recently, most of my inspiration has come from teenagers** who go down to the second-hand shops with a tenner in their pockets and spend hours choosing original combinations of materials, colours and styles. **Let's say I borrow their creativity** and turn it into something softer, less harsh – the kind of thing that wouldn't look out of place at a posh dinner party or a high-class wedding. The thing is, my stuff is so expensive that only a few lucky people can afford it. Anyway, look, you must come and see my new collection. It opens next week.

Speaker 4 **If I were prettier, I'd probably have had a more successful film career.** But you have to admit it, it's easier if you're Catherine Zeta Jones or Julia Roberts, isn't it? A pretty girl once said to me, 'You don't know what prejudice there is against beautiful women'. I think I could put up with that kind of prejudice. **Actually, most of the time I dress for comfort. I'm afraid most of my clothes are pretty messy.** I don't wear anything sleeveless any more, though. My arms are too fat for that now.

Speaker 5 **Basically, it's a wonderful life.** Quite apart from the money, there's the glamour, the fame, the travel. And, on top of all that, I'm paid to wear the kind of clothes most women would kill for. **From that point of view, it's brilliant, but of course there is a downside.** In my situation, if you've got a busy schedule, it can be absolutely exhausting, especially if I'm not eating much because I have to lose a couple of kilos for the next job. And whatever you do, you mustn't let the press attention go to your head. I know that if I want to stay sane, I have to take a break from time to time. I need to get right away from the business, even if it's just for a day or two.

Over to you

Possible answers

People may change their hairstyle or use make-up. They may also change their facial expressions or way of speaking.

Confusing adverbs

3 Key

1	a free	4	a widely
	b freely		b wide
2	a hard	5	a near
	b hardly		b nearly
3	a lately	6	a rough
	b late		b roughly

Vocabulary p51

Lead in

1 Possible answer

Shoes like these are often worn by young people.

Multiple-choice cloze

3 Before students begin the Multiple-choice task, ask them to read the text quickly and answer the following questions: *What nationality was the inventor of Converse shoes?* (American) *What sport were these shoes used for?* (basketball) *What happened in the 1980s and 1990s?* (Converse shoes became less popular) *Who owns Converse now?* (Nike)

Key

1	B	5	A	9	D
2	A	6	C	10	B
3	B	7	A	11	D
4	C	8	C	12	C

Grammar and practice p52

Modal verbs of obligation

1 Key

a don't have to
b must
c must not
d must
e don't need to/needn't
f have to
g mustn't
h need to

2 Key

a sentence h	d sentence f
b sentences d and g	e sentences a and e
c sentences b and c	

3 Key

a didn't have to; won't have to
b had to; will have to
c weren't allowed to; won't be allowed to
d had to; will have to
e didn't need to; won't need to
f had to; will have to
g not possible to change (*mustn't* also refers to the future; there is no past form)
h needed to; will need to

4 Key

1 must/need to
2 needn't
3 mustn't
4 need to
5 should
6 should
7 must
8 should
9 must
10 need to
11 need to/have to

didn't need to/needn't have

6 Encourage students to refer to the Grammar reference on page 179.

Key

Both sentences talk about a lack of obligation, but in sentence b the speaker only realises there was a lack of obligation after the event. The speaker hurried in sentence b.

7 Key

a needn't have driven
b didn't need to go
c didn't need to wash
d needn't have taken
e didn't need to work
f needn't have gone

9 Encourage students to refer to the Grammar reference on page 179.

Cloze

10 Key

1 for
2 because/since
3 or
4 there
5 if/whether
6 what
7 with
8 on
9 it
10 in
11 other
12 all

Exam techniques p54

Reading Part 1

Dos and Don'ts

The exercise that follows introduces the type of multiple-choice exercise which appears in the exam. This section presents some useful strategies for dealing with it. Ask students to read the *Dos and Don'ts*. Check they understand by asking these questions: *Which should you read first, the text or the questions?* (You should read the text quickly first.) *Do you need to read the whole text to answer each question?* (No. Just go to where you think the answer is.)

1 Key

1 B
2 C
3 D
4 C
5 D
6 A
7 C
8 B

Vocabulary p56

Parts of the body

1 Key

a forehead
b eye
c cheek
d jaw
e chin
f neck
g palm
h chest
i knee
j stomach
k shin
l toe
m hand
n wrist
o elbow
p shoulder
q ankle
r waist
s hip
t calf
u leg

2 Key

a shoulder
b toe
c palm
d wrist
e knee
f elbow

Seeing verbs

3 Key

a looks, staring
b watching
c Look
d notice/see
e gazed
f see

Speaking p57

Lead in

1 Background information

1 The Tricorn Centre is in Portsmouth, England. It was designed by Owen Luder and constructed by Taylor Woodrow in the early 1960s. It was a shopping centre and car park and also had some apartments built within it. Originally the building received awards and was considered an exciting example of modern architecture. Public opinion soon turned against it however. It is now empty and waiting to be demolished.

2 The Trellick Tower in West London was designed by the Hungarian architect Erno Goldfinger. Work began on the building in 1968 and was finished four years later. It is a 31 storey, 322 feet high block of flats. In the 1980s it had a terrible reputation for crime and brought the whole idea of high-rise living into disrepute. The reputation of the tower has changed in recent years.

3 The Millennium Dome is in Greenwich, London and was built to celebrate the millennium by housing a huge exhibition. It is the biggest dome in the world, being over 300 metres in diameter and over 50 metres high. It received a lot of criticism, mainly because of its high cost. It cost over £750 million to build.

Long turn

2 Key

a two

b about a minute

c First part: I'd like you to compare the photographs.

Second part: Say how you think the appearance of a city can affect the people who live there.

4 Key

a Yes. She describes one place as 'more beautiful' and the people's lives as 'more stressful'. She also gives details about the differences.

b Yes, she did.

Audioscript

Junko   Yes. OK. So first picture is err like ... I think it might be resort area because beside the river and some ... er I can see kind of castle or something like that. And scenery is ... more beautiful than second one because second one I think is central city somewhere and err tall building and err front of this picture is errr not so beautiful errm ... like a house. I think parents who live in this first picture's area is I think feeling stable because scenery is beautiful maybe they can get the fresh air. But second one is more stress ... or people feel more stressful, erm because I ... just my imagination but maybe this central city it's very busy, traffic is terrible ...

5 While students are doing the task, monitor their discussions and give feedback to the class on their performance. (Did they compare and contrast the photos effectively? Did they answer both parts of the instructions?)

Writing p58

Report

1 Key

a The report will be read by members of the local council.

b The style should be quite formal.

c It is essential to include ideas for things which would attract young people, and how these people can be made aware of these things.

2 Key

a Yes, reports are often written in the passive.

b Yes, suggestions are given.

c the headings (Introduction, Recommendations, Conclusion)

d It is inappropriate to question the council's commitment to actually doing this by saying 'if it really wants to attract people ...'

3 Key

a following ideas <u>should be considered</u> by the local council
rock groups <u>could be invited</u> to play
it <u>is not known</u> to foreign visitors
accommodation <u>could be provided</u>
the town <u>needs to be advertised</u>

b the town's image could be updated

4 Key

    a The old-fashioned hotels *should be replaced with youth hostels instead.*

    b Better sports facilities *should be provided for foreign visitors.*

    c Adverts *could be put in local papers asking for host families where foreign students could stay.*

    d More language schools *could be opened.*

    e An up-to-date website *should be designed.*

Think, plan, write

5 Key

    a the director of the language school

    b It is essential to include suggestions to improve the general appearance of the school.

7 Before students begin to write, encourage them to refer to the Writing guide on page 169.

Overview p60

Key word transformations

1 Key

    1 gave him a job

    2 was taken over by

    3 is responsible for deciding

    4 look like my

    5 needn't have

    6 brought in school uniforms

    7 had his plane landed than

    8 are allowed to leave school

2 Key

    a don't have to go

    b mustn't take

    c needn't have hurried

    d mustn't

    e didn't need to

3 Key

    a puts me off   d put across

    b put on   e put off

    c putting forward

An extra activity to accompany this unit, a unit test and Progress test 1 (Units 1–4) can be downloaded from the Internet at www.oup.com/elt/teacher/exams

5 Foreign parts

Introduction p61

1 Possible answers

a In photo 1, we can see people in Asia dressed in fashions that originate in the West. In photo 2, we can see people in the West using a form of transport most associated with Asia. While the photos show different things, they both show one culture adopting habits from another. Photos 3 and 4 show a similar process in relation to food: Asian people eating Western fast food and Western people eating food from Japan.

Reading p62

Think ahead

2 Check students understand the meaning of the text by asking these questions: *Why didn't the writer travel to New York at first?* (She broke up with her boyfriend and didn't want to travel alone.) *How did the writer feel about travelling?* (excited and nervous) *What made her leave her hotel room?* (seeing the Christmas tree being put up) *How does the writer plan to travel in future?* (mostly alone)

Gapped text

3 You might like to check that students understand the meaning of these words and phrases: *jolt* (a sudden stong feeling), *sob* (the act of crying with sudden, sharp breaths), *wobbly* (not firm or confident), *ushered* (shown where to go), *hoisted* (pulled up into position using ropes), *eased* (moved in slowly and carefully), *lurched* (made a sudden, unsteady movement), *chic* (very fashionable and elegant), *unhindered* (without a person or thing making things difficult).

As the students do the task, encourage them to underline the text that helps them decide on the correct answers.

Key

1 F	3 A	5 G	7 D
2 H	4 C	6 B	

Extra sentence: E

Phrasal verbs: travel

4 Key

a 3	c 1	e 7	g 4
b 5	d 6	f 2	

Grammar and practice p64

Past time

1 Key

a past perfect	c present perfect
b past simple	d past continuous

2 Key

a past perfect	c past simple
b present perfect	d past continuous

3 Encourage students to refer to the Grammar reference on page 180.

Key

1 a past simple
   b past perfect
   In sentence a, the play started just as they arrived. In sentence b, the play started before they arrived at the theatre.

2 a present perfect simple
   b present perfect continuous
   In sentence a, the presents were bought at an unspecified time in the past. In sentence b, the speaker has just returned from buying them and might even be carrying shopping bags.

3 a past continuous
   b past simple
   In sentence a, the speaker was in the act of crossing the road. In sentence b, the speaker

had finished crossing the road before he/she saw Adam.

4 a past simple
b past continuous
In sentence a, she finished filling it out. In sentence b, it's not clear if she has finished filling it out or not.

5 a past simple
b present perfect
In sentence a, he doesn't work for a travel agency anymore. In sentence b, he still works as a travel agent.

4 Ask students to read the text, ignoring the gaps. Check they understand by asking these questions: *What news had the man just heard?* (His wife was having a baby.) *Where did he live?* (Newcastle) *Where was the train he caught going to?* (Edinburgh) *Why was the man upset?* (It didn't stop at Newcastle.) *How did he get off at Newcastle?* (The driver slowed down and the ticket collector lowered him on to the platform.) *What did the guard at the back of the train do?* (He pulled the man back on to the train because he thought he was trying to catch it.)

Key

1 had just had	7 had made
2 was working	8 refused
3 lived	9 held
4 heard	10 dropped
5 was sitting	11 looked
6 was going	12 missed

Participle clauses

5 Key
a Walking up and down the streets in Soho
b Having been repeatedly warned about the ferocity of the customs staff

6 Key
1 b   2 a

7 Encourage the students to refer to the Grammar reference on page 181.

Key
a When/As she was walking down the streets in Soho
b Because/Since she had been repeatedly warned about the ferocity of the customs staff

8 Key
a But, not recognising the man immediately, he said nothing.

b Opening his mouth to ask him what he wanted, Michael suddenly realised who the man was.
c Not having seen his brother since he emigrated to Canada over twenty years ago, Michael hadn't recognised him earlier.
d Having grown a beard, his brother looked quite different.
e Being so pleased to see his brother Patrick, Michael threw his arms around him and hugged him tightly.

Key word transformations

9 Ask students to read the rubric carefully and check they understand what they have to do by asking these questions: *What should you NOT do to the word given?* (change it)

What's the minimum number of words you can use? (two) *What's the maximum number of words you can use?* (five)

Key
1 has been unemployed for
2 when he had peeled/finished peeling
3 not seen Sandra since last
4 leave until she had locked
5 is/has been ages since I enjoyed
6 feeling excited on arrival
7 surprisingly easy to
8 couldn't wait to get
9 took Georgina a long time
10 from feeling tired

Exam techniques p66
Use of English Part 2

Dos and Don'ts
The exercise that follows introduces the type of open cloze which appears in the exam. This section presents some useful strategies for dealing with it. Ask students to read the *Dos and Don'ts*. Check they understand by asking these questions: *Why should you read the text quickly?* (to get a general idea of the topic) *What should you use to help you decide what kind of word is missing?* (the words on either side of the space) *What shouldn't you do?* (leave any spaces empty)

1 Key

1 were	7 in
2 of	8 any
3 around/inside	9 although
4 had	10 bring
5 it/all	11 what
6 to	12 no /few

Vocabulary p67

Lead in

1 When students have read the text make sure they understand the meaning of *etiquette* (an acceptable way of behaving).

Key

impolite, disrespectful, inadvisable, uneducated, indecent, inconsiderate

Negative adjectives

3 Key

immature, dishonest, impossible, inadequate, illogical, unavailable, irrational

1 l	3 p
2 m	4 r

4 Key

inappropriate	disobedient
uncomfortable	impatient
incorrect	immoral
inexpensive	irresponsible
unimportant	unsuccessful
illegal	unsuitable

5 Key

a unsuitable	e irresponsible
b disobedient	f inexpensive
c impatient	g unsuccessful
d illegal	h inappropriate

Exam techniques p68

Listening Part 4

Dos and Don'ts

The exercise that follows introduces a type of task which may appear in Part 4 of the Listening exam. Point out that the task involves selection from two or three possible answers. Ask students to read the *Dos and Don'ts*.

Key

1 B	3 B	5 C	7 B
2 A	4 C	6 A	

Audioscript

Interviewer This afternoon we have in the studio John Reginald, who after many years of serving as a diplomat on behalf of the British government in a large number of countries has decided to retire and devote himself to full-time writing. His first book, which has just been published, is autobiographical and has the title *A strong stomach*. Why this title?

John Reginald Well, food really can be a tricky issue. Obviously, as a diplomat you attend many official dinners and you have to learn to negotiate your way though the minefield of rules of etiquette which must be adhered to. As I'm sure you know every country's culture is different – and what is acceptable in one country or culture can be quite inappropriate in another. But the main thing I discovered very early on in the job is that basically **you really have to be prepared to eat whatever is set in front of you**, and eat it with enthusiasm too. Believe me, that does sometimes necessitate having a strong stomach, hence the title.

Interviewer Can you give us some examples?

John Reginald One that springs to mind, and which I've written about in the book, happened at my first official dinner when I was in my first post, in the Middle East. The main dish was a sheep's head and unfortunately as the guest of honour I was presented with the eyeball, which is regarded over there as a delicacy.

Interviewer Oh, dear! Did you manage to eat it?

John Reginald I didn't really have much choice. If I hadn't eaten it, **I would have offended my hosts.** As simple as that.

Interviewer Hmm, I don't think I could have coped with that even if a diplomatic incident had happened as a result. So was that the worst thing you've ever been served?

John Reginald It was pretty disgusting yes, and among the worst certainly. But there have been many others, I do assure you, that can go into that category. Bat – I had dried bat once when I was in the Pacific Islands – that wasn't very nice either – a bit dry! – needed some gravy – and a bit leathery! It wasn't so much the taste, which was bad enough, but the fact that it was almost impossible to swallow. I seemed to be chewing on it for hours. **But I think top of the list is probably snake blood**, which was served to me at a meal in Thailand. It can be served as a cocktail or just on its own. It might not have been so bad as a cocktail, mixed with something else to disguise the taste.

Interviewer What makes something repulsive to eat?

John Reginald **If I can see what it actually is, it's worse**. If I am obviously eating a part of an animal which is recognisable as such then that makes it harder to eat. If what is on your plate is an eyeball then you can't pretend that you are eating something else. For some people smell is the most important factor but I don't have a very good sense of smell, which has been something of a blessing, and yes, taste is important as well. I'm thinking of the raw turtle eggs I ate in Nicaragua. They were fishy, in an extremely unpleasant way.

Interviewer So what advice would you give to someone in a situation where something is put in front of them that they don't want to eat?

John Reginald I'd say: one, don't not eat it. You need to be polite. It could be one of their national dishes. Two, take it easy; eat too fast and you might find that you get some more and, three, **pretend you're eating something you like**.

Interviewer The book is doing very well, I believe. I understand it's come in at number twenty on the bestsellers list. You must be very pleased.

John Reginald I'm absolutely delighted.

Interviewer **I have to say that I found it very amusing.** From the title I thought it was going to be some sort of medical textbook, so I was pleasantly surprised. Is there another book in the pipeline?

John Reginald Yes, but the next one will be totally different. My editor wanted me to do a follow-up to this one – again based on my experiences – things that went wrong and almost led to diplomatic incidents.

And I had thought about doing a sort of guide book for businessmen who travel abroad – etiquette in different countries – there's a definite market for that especially with the growth of China. **But I've recently become very interested in the origins and rationale behind the consumption of food in different countries so that's what it'll be about.** Did you know that ...

Vocabulary p69

Lead in

1 Key

a It is unacceptable not to finish your serving of rice.

Confusing words

2 Key

dishes (*plates* is the crockery that food is served in)

pair (*pair* is used to talk about two things which are specifically used together, e.g. a left and right shoe make a pair; *couple* simply means two of something)

raises (*rises* means to get higher, rather than move something up)

3 Key

a recipe
b fast
c junk
d tap, still
e savoury
f cook
g menu, list

1 Write pairs of definitions on the board. Ask students to identify the words.

1 a water that has never had bubbles
  b a fizzy drink that has lost its bubbles
2 a instructions to make a dish
  b piece of paper that shows what you've bought
3 a eat certain food for a period of time to lose weight
  b eat nothing for a period of time for religious reasons
4 a word used to describe hamburgers, chips, etc.
  b things you don't want to keep
5 a items of food available in a restaurant
  b types of wine available in a restaurant
6 a somebody who cooks food
  b something you cook food on

(Answers: 1 a still b flat; 2 a recipe b receipt; 3 a diet b fast; 4 a fast b rubbish; 5 a menu b list; 6 a cook b cooker)

2 Students use the words to make up sentences.

Extreme adjectives

4 Key

tiny

5 Encourage students to refer to the Grammar reference on page 181.

Key

hilarious – funny
boiling – hot
delicious – tasty
amazed – impressed/surprised
filthy – dirty
huge – big/large
terrified – scared/afraid/frightened
delighted – happy/pleased
freezing – cold
exhausted – tired
spotless – clean
furious – angry

6 Key

a boiling	d angry, hilarious
b small	e delighted
c spotless	f delicious

Listening p70

Think ahead

1 Possible answers

Other reasons for going to other countries include: to experience another culture; to get a suntan; to see the landscape and wildlife; to teach a language or another skill; to see or participate in a sporting event.

Multiple matching

2 Key

a		b	
Speaker 1	Australia	Speaker 1	positive
Speaker 2	Spain	Speaker 2	negative
Speaker 3	USA	Speaker 3	positive
Speaker 4	Norway	Speaker 4	positive
Speaker 5	France	Speaker 5	positive

Audioscript

Speaker 1 I've been in Australia for a month now and I've really enjoyed it. It's just so different. My sister keeps telling me I should consider moving out here but I'm not sure. Obviously it would be nice to be able to see more of her. **This is the first time I've seen her in five years.** I don't get to see her that often just because it's so expensive to get here. I can't really imagine what it would be like to actually live here on a permanent basis. Sydney's a lovely city but I'm not sure if I'd want to settle down here. I think I'd miss being so far away from Europe. But who knows?

Speaker 2 Why did I come to Spain? Well, as far as my parents are concerned I came here to learn Spanish. **The real reason though was that I fancied something a bit different.** You know what it's like - when you've lived all your life in one place it gets a bit 'samey'. I can't say I know much about Spain or the people yet, though. I'm working here as an au pair, and I've got three children to look after, all under six. So, even when I have some free time, I don't have much energy to go out. I don't speak much Spanish yet either because everyone I meet wants to practise their English. What can you do?

Speaker 3 I was a bit tired when I arrived – I couldn't sleep on the plane unfortunately. John picked me up at the airport and **took me to the office. We had a short meeting to sort out the finances,** and then I took a taxi straight to the hotel. It's a great place. I'm on the thirty-first floor, so I've got a pretty good view of the city centre.

The White House is just a few blocks away, apparently. And it's got all the usual stuff: air-conditioning, satellite TV. You wouldn't believe the bed though, it's absolutely huge.

Speaker 4   I'd been to Norway on holiday on several occasions but, ironically, I met Thomas when I was in the States, having an operation. He was working as a nurse in the same hospital. We kept in touch after I came home, and then I came over to Norway again the following summer. **We got engaged almost immediately and had a church wedding a few months later.** We'll actually be celebrating our second anniversary this October. I've never regretted coming here and I don't think we'd ever consider moving. The lifestyle is better – it's much less stressful. Maybe the people are a bit cold at first, but once you get to know them they're really nice.

Speaker 5   I did it at school but the teaching methods were so old-fashioned that I never got very far with it. I remember I had a pen-friend when I was sixteen and went over to France for a month and couldn't even ask the way. Yet I could read poetry in French. How ridiculous is that! **So this time round I decided the only way to really get to grips with it was to go to the country and spend a few months there.** I didn't bother with classes because I didn't want any formal teaching. I just really wanted to surround myself with French and immerse myself in it. And it worked. I'm much more fluent now than I was.

3 Key

Speaker 1	F	Speaker 4	A
Speaker 2	E	Speaker 5	D
Speaker 3	C		

The extra statement is B.

Phrasal verbs with *look*

4 Key

a	7	d	6	f	2
b	5	e	1	g	3
c	4				

Speaking p71

Two-way task

2 This task is another example of Part 3 of the Speaking exam. Check students understand the task by asking the following questions: *What do the pictures show?* (ways of getting to know a country) *What should you do first?* (talk about what you can learn from each experience) *What should you do after that?* (decide which two experiences you would most enjoy)

If you feel the students need ideas, go through one or two of the photos with the class. For example ask: *What does the first picture show?* (people sightseeing) *What could you learn about a country from this experience?* (something about the country's history, culture, and architecture)

Before students begin, ask them to read the information in the tip box. Check they understand by asking the following questions: *What should you do together?* (try to reach an agreement) *How should you do this?* (each make suggestions about different options and say why you'd choose them)

Monitor students as they do the task and give feedback to the class when they have finished. (Did they talk about what they might learn from each experience? Did they listen to each other properly? Did they make proper suggestions about why they might choose a particular option? Did they come to an agreement?)

Possible answers

As a volunteer on an *archaeological* dig, you could learn about the people who lived in a country in the past and how the history of the country was shaped.

From *doing voluntary work* you could learn about the problems that people in that country face while meeting lots of the locals on a personal level.

By *working as an au pair*, you could learn a lot about family life in another culture, as well as having lots of opportunities to learn the local language.

From *learning a language* you could learn a lot about the culture and be able to participate in it, as well as discovering the country's literature.

On a *backpacking* holiday you could learn about the geography of a country and find out about the natural environment.

Discussion

3 These discussion questions represent the type of questions that students are asked to discuss in Part 4 of the Speaking exam. They relate to the topic of Part 3.

Writing p72

Informal letter

1 Key

a The letter will be read by your penfriend.
b The purpose is to describe a festival you know.
c The tone should be friendly.

2 Key

a Yes. The letter describes a festival in Agnés's home town.
b Yes. Agnés uses a familiar tone, contractions, and phrases such as 'Drop me a line'.
c Yes. Agnés doesn't use formal phrases like 'Dear …' and 'Yours faithfully'.

Creating interest

3 Key

1 d	3 e	5 b
2 c	4 a	

4 Key

interest in the other person: b, d
making the letter more descriptive: a, c, e

5 Key

1 briskly
2 crowds of
3 cheering
4 scarlet and black
5 shiny
6 enormous

Think, plan, write

6 Encourage students to refer to the Writing guide on page 164.

Key

a The letter should start with 'Hi' or 'Hello' and go on to ask how your friend is.
b Include information about where, when and why the festival takes place. Describe some features and tell your friend about parts you think they would find interesting.

Overview p74

1 Key

1	were	7	to
2	where	8	as
3	as	9	well
4	who/that	10	there
5	the	11	while/whereas/but
6	with	12	of

2 Key

a

1	hadn't rung	5	found
2	got	6	was lying
3	rushed	7	had packed
4	had left		

b

1 have ever ridden
2 sat
3 seemed

c

1	happened	4	was listening
2	was travelling	5	was lying
3	was driving	6	had crashed

3 Key

a	up	e	off
b	over	f	off/out
c	up	g	forward
d	in, round	h	after

An extra activity to accompany this unit and a unit test can be downloaded from the Internet at www.oup.com/elt/teacher/exams

6 The mind

Introduction p75

1 Key

Items 1 and 2 test IQ. Items 3 and 4 test EQ.

1 c

2 e

3 a represents the highest EQ

4 b represents the highest EQ

2 Possible answers

a Tests like these might be useful for employers trying to find the right staff. However, creative and artistic abilities are not tested.

b It has been shown that practising IQ tests can improve your score. Similarly for EQ tests, it can help to know what kind of answer is expected.

Listening p76

Think ahead

1 Encourage students to think of positive and negative influences. For example, a caring upbringing may lead to confidence in later life. However, uninterested parents may cause low self-esteem and a tendency to fail.

Sentence completion

2 Key

a four-year-olds and insurance salesmen

b It seemed to prove that EQ is as important as IQ when determining success. The research showed that self-control as a young child led to a higher IQ and greater social confidence in adolescents. The research also showed that naturally optimistic salesmen performed better at work and were less likely to leave their jobs.

Audioscript

Woman The idea that women feel whereas men think, and that thinking is somehow superior to feeling, is an attitude that some people would now consider out of date. Many of today's psychologists argue that emotional intelligence is just as important as IQ when determining a person's overall success. Let me give you some examples of research which backs up this theory. When ninety-five graduates from Harvard University were followed into middle age, **the men with the highest intelligence test scores in college were not found to be particularly successful** – in terms of salary, productivity or status – compared with those who had scored lower. **IQ it would seem, contributes only about 20% to the factors that determine life success, leaving 80% to other forces.** So what are these other forces? Peter Salovey of Yale University would argue that **emotional self-control is one of the most important.** He conducted an experiment with a class of four-year-olds. He gave each of them a sweet and told them they could eat it immediately. **However, if they could resist eating it until the experimenter came back into the classroom, he would then give them two sweets.** For what seemed like an endless fifteen minutes, most of the children waited. In their struggle to resist the sweet, they put their hands over their eyes, talked to themselves, sang, and even tried to go to sleep. **About a third of the children were unable to wait.** They grabbed the sweet almost immediately the experimenter left the room. **When the same children were followed up as teenagers,** those who at four had been able to resist temptation were, as **adolescents,** more socially competent, self-reliant, dependable and confident. **They also had dramatically higher scores on IQ tests.** However, those who at four had been unable to resist temptation were more indecisive, more socially isolated and less confident. This experiment suggests that emotional self-control is an important contributor to intellectual potential, quite apart from IQ itself. **Another ability that can determine not just academic but job success is optimism.** In a study of insurance salesmen, psychologist Martin Seligman showed the relation between optimism and high work performance. Selling insurance is a difficult job, and three quarters of insurance salesmen leave in their first three years. **Given the high costs of recruiting and training,** the emotional state of new employees has become an economic issue for insurance companies. Seligman's study found that new salesmen who were natural optimists sold 37% more in their first two years than salesmen who were **pessimists, and were much less likely to leave in the first year.** Why was optimism so important in that situation? Because people who are pessimists explain failures as due to some permanent characteristic in themselves or in others that they cannot change. Optimists on the other hand explain failures as due to something temporary that can be changed. So they believe they can succeed next time round.

3 Remind students that they should read through the sentences before listening. They should try to work out what kind of word is missing by looking at the words before and after the gap.

Optional activity

Before students do task 3, ask them to read the sentences and to predict the kind of word(s) that is likely to fill the gap. (Answers: a adjective – part of a comparative sentence; b more + adjective; c noun – relates to *factors*; d noun; e a quantity; f plural noun – relates to *children*; g noun; h noun – relates to *factor*; i verb; j plural noun)

Key
a successful
b more important
c emotional self-control
d two sweets
e a/one third
f teenagers/adolescents
g higher scores
h optimism
i recruit and train
j Pessimists

Personal qualities

4 Key

Positive
confident – confidence
dependable – dependability
self-reliant – self-reliance

Negative
indecisive – indecision
pessimistic – pessimism/pessimist

5 Key

a indecisive	d dependable
b confidence	e Pessimists
c self-reliant	

Grammar and practice p77

Gerunds

1 Encourage students to refer to the Grammar reference on page 181.

Key
a Thinking 1; feeling 2
b eating 3/2
c Selling 1
d training 4

2 Key

a Having	d Writing
b Remembering	e Forgetting
c Repeating/saying	

3 Key
a at remembering/at memorising
b of memorising/of remembering
c in improving
d about having
e for reminding

4 Possible answers

be mad about, adore, love, enjoy, be keen on, be interested in, like.
dislike, have an aversion to, can't stand, can't bear, hate, detest, loathe.

Gerunds and infinitives

6 Key

a to catch	f to play
b to meet	g to lend
c changing	h driving
d to be	i to understand
e losing	j to buy

7 Encourage students to refer to the Grammar reference on page 182.

Key

3 b	6 a	9 b
4 a	7 a	10 a
5 b	8 b	

8 Key

a to get/to buy/to bring
b to announce
c to open/opening
d chatting/speaking/fidgeting
e agreeing
f eating
g leaving

Key word transformations

9 Key

1 can't stand people interrupting
2 arriving in time
3 no good at remembering / not (very) good at remembering
4 have ('ve) arranged to meet John
5 couldn't afford to go

Speaking p79

Lead in

1 Possible answer

Stress can result in problems in relationships, poor health, an increase in the use of substances such as alcohol and tobacco, altered eating habits, a decrease in the quality of work, and psychological difficulties.

Two-way task

2 Ask students to read the tip. Check they understand by asking the following question: *How can you encourage your partner to speak?* (by asking them a question)

Key

a Yes, both questions are answered.
b Yes. The following questions are included:
   And do you think it would be good ...?
   How about ...?
   Why?
   Do you like ...?
   So which activities will we choose ...?
   How about you?
   What do you think about that?
c They make interjections such as *yes/yeah*. They ask and answer questions. They agree and disagree with points that are made.

Audioscript

Sophie	OK the first picture shown. It shows a man who does exercise on something. And **do you think it would be good** in an article?
Jay	Yes, I think exercise is a very good practice err to relieve the stress, because when I ... when I was exercising I forgot every the stress ... any stress. Yes. Sometime ... and it ... when you swear ... sweat you forget everything, I think. So it is good for your re ... good for relieving your stress.
Sophie	I think I would prefer yoga because it's (Yeah). I never did it but I heard a lot about it and it should be really relaxing. And you concentrate on your own and your energy and the flowed of your blood and (Yes right) your breathing I think that would relax me more than doing sports and exercises.
Jay	Err ... **How about** having a bath?
Sophie	Pardon?
Jay	Mm. **How about** having a bath?
Sophie	Have ... Yes, I like that too.
Jay	Yes, **why?**
Sophie	Because in the evening if you, if you had a hard day and you come home and take a warm bath it's ... it's very nice. (Yeah) You could also listen to music. **Do you like** listening to music for relaxing? (Yes)
Jay	Yeah yeah for relaxing yes. Sometimes I listen to music especially the rock music, very heavy music, because because erm when I heard the rock music or the heavy metal music I dreamed about my ideal place so I prefer listen to music ... to relieve the stress.

Sophie	Yes. If I listen to music most of the time I'm painting besides. Because I ... for me music is not something ... a main activity. I can just do it besides and I like painting a lot because you concentrate on something but (Oh yes) your thoughts can throw away and you can daydream.
Jay	Yeah. I really want to paint, I really want to paint but I can't because I never tried painting. How about going on holiday?
Sophie	Yeah, It's very good but you need time.
Jay	Yes, you need time and you need the money.
Sophie	Yes. **So which activities will we choose** for our article?
Jay	I want to choose the exercise, and err painting and the listen to music. **How about** (Yeah) **you?**
Sophie	Yeah, I think these are the very common ones. Probably going on holiday we could erm replace for painting. (Yes) Cos it's very well known and painting is just something ... not not many people do to ... do paint but everybody's going on holidays I think. (Yes, like) It would attract more people to read the article. **What do you think about that?**

3 Monitor students as they do the task and give feedback to the class at the end. (Did they listen to each other properly? How did they show this? Did one person dominate or did they have an equal discussion? Did they ask each other questions to keep the conversation going? Did they complete both questions?)

Possible answers

Exercise might help people to relax by getting rid of surplus energy.

Going on holiday might help people to relax by offering a change in environment and opportunities to do different things in the fresh air.

Yoga is said to decrease tension and make people more calm in their everyday lives.

Having a bath might help relax muscles and provide warmth and a pleasant smell. It can also leave you feeling fresher.

Painting and other creative hobbies demand concentration which takes your mind off work and other sources of stress.

Listening to music, especially calm music, can take you away from the unpleasant noises and stresses of the world around you.

Discussion

4 Possible answers
  a People may be more stressed than in the past because of job insecurity and a rapidly changing world.
  b Companies could make work more relaxing by allowing longer holidays, providing a welcoming environment, and encouraging employees to talk about their problems at work.
  c It might be a bad thing to be too relaxed in a job which demands a strong sense of responsibility, especially if the operation of dangerous equipment is required.

Exam techniques p80

Reading Part 2

Dos and Don'ts

The exercise that follows introduces the type of gapped text which appears in the exam. This section presents some useful strategies for dealing with it. Ask students to read the *Dos and Don'ts*. Check they understand by asking these questions: *What is missing from a gapped text?* (whole sentences) *What parts of the text can help you decide on the correct option?* (reference words and other language connections)

When they have finished choosing their correct options, ask students to justify their decisions by underlining reference words and language connections.

1 Key

1 F	3 E	5 B	7 C
2 H	4 D	6 G	

Extra sentence: A

Vocabulary p82

Collocation

4 Key

a soundly	b face	c deepest

5 Key

a close	d heavy	f heavy
b serious	e serious	g strong
c hard		

6 Key

argue passionately
drink heavily
listen attentively
sleep soundly
think hard
work hard

7 Key

a ~~performing~~   c ~~say~~
b ~~acquire~~   d ~~making~~

Optional activity

1 Write the following words from the vocabulary
sections in two columns and ask students to match
them to form collocations.

1	find	a	crime
2	strong	b	friend
3	face	c	rain
4	close	d	soundly
5	serious	e	an opinion
6	sleep	f	wind
7	heavy	g	a problem
8	express	h	a solution

(Answers: 1 h   2 f   3 g   4 b   5 a   6 d   7 c   8 e)

2 Students use the collocations to write sentences.

Multiple-choice cloze

8 Ask students to find words in the text that have
these meanings: repairs (*maintenance*), increase
(*build up*), to a degree, partly (*to some extent*), fall
asleep (*drop off*), move about quickly (*twitch*),
ideas that haven't been proved (*theories*).

Check students understand the text by asking the
following questions: *What's the average number
of hours we sleep during our lifetime?* (twenty
years) *How does sleep help our bodies to heal?*
(during sleep all energy is channelled for one
purpose – healing) *What keeps us awake?*
(caffeine) *What causes us to sleep?*(alcohol and
some medicines) *What do scientists use to
monitor what is happening when we sleep?*
(electrodes) *At what point do we normally dream?*
(after ninety minutes of sleep) *What is REM?*
(Rapid Eye Movement)

Key

1	C	5	B	9	D
2	D	6	C	10	C
3	A	7	C	11	B
4	D	8	A	12	D

Writing p84

Short story

3 Key

2	C	4	B	6	E	8	D
3	F	5	A	7	H		

4 Key

A	politely	E	Patiently
B	noticeably	F	carefully
D	Furiously		

Dramatic effect

5 Possible answers

Paragraph 1: I shouted angrily; … shrugged her
shoulders casually … / walked casually …
Paragraph 2: … briskly walked across the road/
walked briskly across the road; hurriedly
straightening my tie …
Paragraph 3: … looked strangely familiar …
Paragraph 4: Reluctantly opening the envelope, …
/Opening the envelope reluctantly …

6 Key

a He dashed across the road.
b She whispered the answer.
c The traffic crawled through the town centre.
d He crept upstairs.
e She yelled, 'Look out!'
f They strolled through the park arm in arm.

Think, plan, write

8 Encourage students to refer to the Writing guide
on page 172.

Overview p86

1 Key

1 actually	6 knowledge
2 telepathic	7 sensible
3 correctly	8 inconsistent
4 hardly	9 extraordinary
5 limited	10 scientific

2 Key

a to post	e using
b clearing	f to get
c dealing, to work	g meeting
d to say	h moving

3 Key

a soundly	e heavy
b strong, strong	f came up with
c severe	g strong
d make	

An extra activity to accompany this unit and a unit test can be downloaded from the Internet at www.oup.com/elt/teacher/exams

7 Free time

Introduction

This discussion is based on the students' own answers. Encourage the students to make comparisons between themselves and the people shown in the pictures 1–5.

Reading p88

2 Ask students to find words in the text that mean: say definitely (*guarantee*), bring up (*rear*), changed from something else (*converted*), consider why something happens (*analyse*), hard work (an expression) (*elbow grease*), logical way of thinking (*common sense*), a sport involving running across country with a map (*orienteering*), calming (*soothing*).

Multiple matching

3 Key

1	G
2	B
3, 4	A, D
5	C
6, 7	B, F
8, 9, 10	E, F, G
11	B
12	G
13	C
14	D
15	A

Prefixes

4 Key

a *co-habiting* means living together; *co-* means together
b *pre-booked* means the reservation was made at an earlier time; *pre-* means before
c *detoxifying* means getting rid of poisons and toxins, *revitalising* means making more lively and energetic; *de-* means taking away, *re-* means doing again

5 Key

a 4	c 2	e 3
b 6	d 1	f 5

6 Key

a postgraduate
b ex-president
c antifreeze
d underground
e midnight
f semi-detached

Grammar and practice p90

Passive verbs

1 Key

a Weekends <u>are filled</u> (passive – Present simple passive) with the fun of the farm, and appetites <u>are satisfied</u> (passive - Present simple passive) with delicious home-cooked local food.
b Residential weekends <u>are held</u> (passive – Present simple passive) throughout the year.
c You <u>will be instructed</u> (passive – Future simple passive) on how to produce local cheese.
d <u>Learn</u> (active – Present simple) how to build a wheel, which you <u>can</u> (active – Present simple) take away at the end.
e All the activities <u>can be pre-booked</u> (passive – Present simple passive) or <u>chosen</u> (passive – Present simple passive) on the day.

2 Key

The passive is formed with *be* in the appropriate tense (present, past, etc.) and the past participle of the main verb.

3 Key

a We fill the weekends with the fun of the farm, and we satisfy your appetites with delicious home-cooked local food.

b We hold residential weekends throughout the year.

c We will instruct you on how to produce local cheese.

d You will be taught how to build a wheel, which can be taken away at the end.

e You can either pre-book any of the activities or choose them on the day.

The focus of the sentence changes depending on whether it is active or passive, for example in sentence *a* the focus in the passive is on the actions, whereas in the active the focus is on the people who perform the actions.

4 Key

a the experts

b the unpaid volunteers

5 Encourage students to refer to the Grammar reference on page 183.

Key

a the owners of the farm

b the owners of the farm

c the instructor

d the participants

e the participants

We are not told who performs the action for one of the following reasons: it is not known, it's obvious, it's not necessary to know, or the person has already been mentioned.

6 Key

1	is guaranteed	6	is included
2	is located	7	is served
3	are furnished	8	be booked
4	are equipped	9	will be made
5	are reserved		

7 Key

You have won an all-expenses paid weekend for two in London.

You will be met at Heathrow airport by one of our chauffeurs and driven into central London. You will be put up in a five-star hotel close to Harrods, the world's most famous department store. A luxury suite has been reserved for you on the tenth floor. In addition to this, you will be given £1,000 'pocket money'. This money can be spent as you like.

Have/get something done

8 Key

a The person whose birthday it was took the photos.

b An unspecified person or people at the party took photos.

c The person whose birthday it was asked somebody to take photos for him/her.

9 Key

In sentence a, the tooth was filled with the person's agreement, but in sentence b the stealing of the car was something which was out of their control.

Encourage students to refer to the Grammar reference on page 184.

10 Key

b I got/had my hair cut in a completely different style.

c We've had our apartment repainted.

d I'm going to have my video repaired next week.

e I'm having my jacket cleaned.

f The council has had the town hall rebuilt.

11 Possible answers

a You can have/get your teeth cleaned, pulled out, or filled.

b People go to the hairdresser's to have/get their hair cut, permed, washed, or dyed.

c People take their cars to garages to have/get them repaired or serviced.

d You could have/get your hair cut or have/get some plastic surgery done.

Cloze

13 Key

1	not	7	ask
2	than	8	for
3	soon	9	with
4	if	10	pay
5	Make	11	yourself
6	over/around	12	well

Vocabulary p92

Lead in

1 Key

a Finalist let down by unreliable serve (tennis)
b Slam-dunk wins game (basketball)
c Three holes to win The US Open (golf)
d Fans riot after heavyweight knocked out in first round (boxing)
e Keeper gets red card three minutes after kick-off (football)
f Gold for British sprinter (athletics)
g Vital seconds lost in handlebar mix-up (cycling)
h Disaster after pit stop for wheel change (motor-racing)

Get students to say which words in the headlines helped them to make their choices:

a serve
b slam-dunk
c holes/The US Open
d heavyweight/knocked out/first round
e keeper/red card/kick-off
f Gold/sprinter
g handlebar
h pit stop/wheel change

Sports vocabulary

2 Key

Someone who plays tennis is a tennis player.
Someone who plays football is a footballer.
Someone who plays golf is a golfer.
Someone who goes motor-racing is a racing driver.
Someone who goes cycling is a cyclist.
Someone who boxes is a boxer.
Someone who does athletics is an athlete.
Someone who plays basketball is a basketball player.

3 Possible answers

football: football, football boots, net
golf: golf clubs, golf balls, tee
motor-racing: racing car, crash helmet
cycling: bike, helmet
boxing: gloves, shorts
athletics: starting blocks, starting pistol
basketball: basketball, basketball nets

4 Possible answers

on a pitch – football
on a course – golf
on a court – tennis, basketball, badminton, volleyball
on a circuit – cycling, motor-racing
on a (race) track – horse-racing, athletics
in a pool – swimming, diving
in a gym – weight-lifting
in a ring – boxing, wrestling
in a rink – ice-skating

5 Key

1 a	3 c	5 b
2 d	4 b	6 a

Optional activity

Give students the following definitions and ask them to identify them with words from the vocabulary sections:

1 You play football here.
2 It's where a racing car stops to refuel.
3 Somebody who runs a short distance very quickly.
4 It's where you go ice-skating.
5 It's what you do when you try to take the ball from somebody in football.
6 The first hit of a ball in tennis is called this.
7 It's where boxing takes place.
8 It's the name of the beginning of a football match.

(Answers: 1 pitch; 2 pit stop; 3 sprinter; 4 rink; 5 tackle; 6 serve; 7 ring; 8 kick-off)

Exam techniques p93

Listening Part 2

Dos and Don'ts

The exercise that follows introduces the type of completion task that appears in the Listening exam. Explain that students will be asked to complete whole sentences. Ask students to read the *Dos and Don'ts*. Check they understand by asking the following questions: *What should you do when you read the sentences?* (decide what kind of information you'll be listening for) *What's the maximum number of words you should write?* (three)

Key

1 crossword puzzle
2 craze
3 Maths
4 train
5 effort
6 addicted
7 (really) difficult
8 communicating
9 her boyfriend
10 competitions

Audioscript

Interviewer Hi Charlie. In case there's anyone listening who doesn't know what Sudoku is, can you just to explain it very simply, please.

Charlie Sure. **It's a bit like a crossword puzzle** but with numbers not words. You have to fill the numbers one to nine in a square grid. Each vertical and horizontal line has to include the numbers one to nine once each. To make it easier, some of the numbers are filled in for you and you have to work out what the rest are.

Interviewer OK, enough, enough. I'm already confused. What I really want to ask you is this. What on earth do you see in Sudoku? I mean, I know **it's a craze that's been sweeping the country – probably the world** – in the last two or three years, but all you have to do is fill in squares with numbers. And when you've finished, you do another one. What makes it so enjoyable?

Charlie Well, for a start I should tell you that you don't have to be good at Maths to enjoy Sudoku – **I was always useless at Maths when I was at school.** As far as why I enjoy it goes, that's a difficult question. You may understand it better if I tell you when and where I usually do it. The thing is on my way to and from work **I spend quite a lot of my time on trains – and to me that's dead time – the perfect time for Sudoku.** The time just flies by.

Interviewer OK, I realise that being on a train can be boring, but surely there are other things you could, like reading a book or a newspaper or chatting to other passengers?

Charlie **No – reading and chatting take too much effort.** I mean you have to concentrate on Sudoku but you don't have to think deeply – and that means you can switch your brain off and relax. I suppose it's a kind of therapy which helps to keep me sane.

Interviewer Have you always enjoyed doing puzzles?

Charlie No, not at all. I've never really been interested in puzzles of any kind. When Sudoku came on the scene, I just couldn't see the point of it. More and more people I knew started doing it. It was in all the newspapers and magazines and on the Internet – you just couldn't get away from it. I assumed I wouldn't be able to do it because it's all numbers. I resisted it for as long as I could, but then **one of my friends, who was completely obsessed with it, persuaded me to try it. And that was it – two games later I was addicted to it.**

Interviewer And is it something you can get better at?

Charlie Yes, of course. When I started, even the simplest puzzle would take me 20 minutes or more. **Now I can do the really difficult ones in about ten minutes.**

Interviewer But doesn't it worry you that it's such an anti-social hobby? You're sort of locked up in your own little world, aren't you? **Cynics might say it was a way for anti-social people to make sure they never had to bother communicating.**

Charlie There is a danger of that, I suppose, but it doesn't have to be a solitary occupation. **My boyfriend and I play it together sometimes.**

Interviewer You mean you work on the same puzzle at the same time?

Charlie Yes, we have done that, but now **we have little competitions where we see which of us can finish a puzzle first.** And we've done it with larger groups of people as well. We've even been to a Sudoku party!

Interviewer Sounds terrible. Anyway Charlie, thanks. I've really enjoyed meeting you and discovering some of the mysteries of Sudoku. I'm afraid you haven't convinced me to try it, but I think I understand now why some people are so keen on it. Thanks.

Speaking p94

Lead in

1 Possible answer

Essential items could include a tent, a sleeping bag, a torch, a camping stove, cutlery, and a ground mat.

Two-way task

2 Ask the following questions: *How many parts does the task have?* (two) *What are they?* (talk about how useful each item is; agree on which two things to take) *How can you encourage your partner to speak?* (by asking questions) *How can you show you are listening?* (by agreeing and disagreeing appropriately; making interjections)

While students are doing the task, monitor their discussions and give feedback to the class about their performance. (Did they complete both parts of the task effectively? Did they listen to each other? Did they both speak?)

Possible answers

A *radio* might be useful for keeping in touch with what is happening in the news and for playing music, provided that the reception was good.

A *kite* would be useful if there were children in your party and also as a form of relaxation, but using it would depend on the weather.

A *computer* could be useful if you need to complete some work or if you want to use email. However, you would need to be able to recharge the battery easily and it might be heavy to transport.

A *football* would be useful for keeping fit and avoiding boredom. It does not require another energy source.

A *coffee-maker* would be useful for fresh coffee, provided that you had a camping stove on which to heat it.

A *chess set* would be useful for keeping your mind active. It does not require another energy source and is easy to transport.

A *book* would help avoid boredom. It is easy to carry and does not require an energy source.

Discussion

3 Remind students that Part 4 of the Speaking exam involves discussing questions related to the theme of Part 3.

Key

a cooking outside
b taking a bath
c a quiet campsite full of smiling people

Audioscript

Thorkild	What do you enjoy most and least about camping?
Megumi	Camping? Erm I think **I enjoy cooking outside**.
Thorkild	If you go camping, do you prefer to stay in one place or move from place to place?
Fabienne	I prefer move from place to place to ...
Thorkild	Why?
Fabienne	To discover the country which I visit.
Thorkild	When you go camping, what do you miss most from your 'normal' life?
Megumi	Err ... **Maybe taking a bath**, I think. I really like it.
Thorkild	Why?
Megumi	Because it ... Taking a bath makes me relaxing. Yeah so ... Maybe if ... If I go to camping it's only taking a shower, so I ... I think I need it.
Thorkild	What is your idea of a perfect campsite?
Fabienne	My perfect idea of a campsite is **really quiet and where the people are erm smiling and not stressed** because sometime I think in camping some people wait for the shower, the toilet and and they almost fight together and I don't, I don't like really camping.
Thorkild	What is the most popular type of holiday in your country?
Megumi	Maybe going to travel abroad, I think ... and err ... or go to hot spring – it's very popular in Japan and I really like it.
Thorkild	Which areas of your country do holiday-makers and tourists visit?
Fabienne	I think this is the mountains – we have the famous Alps in Switzerland and a lot of people are going to ski. And I think this is ... is really famous for that because the landscape is beautiful.
Thorkild	Thank you. That is the end of the test.

4 Possible answer

Megumi uses *Maybe* a lot in her answer. This is probably because she lacks fluency when speculating about a subject. She could use phrases like *Perhaps* or *Possibly*. Alternatively, she could use modal verbs such as *could*, *may* or *might* in her sentences.

5 Ask students to read the tip box. Check they have understood by asking *How can you improve your answers?* (give reasons and explanations for your opinions)

While students are doing the task, monitor their discussions and give feedback to the class about their performance. (Did they express their opinions clearly? Did they give good reasons for their opinions? Did they listen to each other's ideas appropriately?)

Exam techniques p95

Use of English Part 1

Dos and Don'ts

The exercise that follows introduces the type of multiple-choice cloze task which appears in the Listening exam. Ask students to read the *Dos and Don'ts*. Check they understand by asking the following question: *What can help you decide on the correct choice?* (the words on either side of the space)

1 Ask students to read the text and to decide on the meaning of the title *Recharge your batteries* (take a rest so that you can continue working well).

Key

1	D	5	B	9	A
2	B	6	D	10	B
3	B	7	A	11	A
4	D	8	D	12	C

Vocabulary

Phrasal verbs with *come*

1 Key

a came along	e came forward
b came apart	f has come up
c come across	g come round
d came round	h comes up with

Which word?

3 Key

a possibility	f stop	k peak
b method	g fewer	l height
c choice	h minor	m surplus
d pause	i less	n excess
e rest	j top	o spare

Listening p97

Lead in

1 Possible answers

a Other kinds of music might include rock, hip-hop, folk, dance, pop, easy listening, reggae, etc.

b Situations might include: in nightclubs, at the gym, in shops, while travelling, etc.

c People might listen to music for relaxation, dancing, or because they are studying music.

Multiple choice

2 Remind students to read and think about the questions before they listen to the recording.

Key

1	C	3	A	5	C	7	B
2	C	4	B	6	B	8	C

Audioscript

1

Man **Definitely jazz – any kind really – traditional or modern.** I don't exactly know what it is about it that appeals to me. It's not just the music; it's the atmosphere in the clubs and the people you meet at concerts. I quite like other kinds of music as well: blues, soul, world, even some classical. But I have to say, I'm not that keen on pop. It all sounds the same to me these days – a sure sign that I'm getting middle-aged.

2

Woman It was amazing. My friend and me were right at the front. We were in the most expensive seats. But even there it was almost impossible to hear anything. **As soon as they came on and started playing, everyone went mad. You could just about hear the bass and the drums** from time to time, but the words were completely inaudible. We could see their mouths opening and closing, but nothing seemed to come out.

3

Woman It's everywhere you go these days. I was on the train on the way to work last week. **A girl came and sat next to me. I was trying to read a report and all I could hear was this repetitive drumming noise** – sort of disco music, I suppose. I just couldn't concentrate. **I've got a friend who listens when he goes jogging.** That's OK, because he's not disturbing anyone. But in public places **they're a real nuisance** – a blatant case of noise pollution if you ask me.

4

Man **I've got an email here from Mrs Johnson. She'd like to have** *Love Hurts* **played for her son Michael.** Mum sends you her love, Michael, wherever you are. She's asked me to tell you that she loves you very much and says please, please, please contact her before your birthday – she doesn't want to lose touch with you. Just a phone call would do. You don't have to tell her where you are if you don't want to. So, for Michael Johnson, here's *Love Hurts* from your Mum.

5

Man **I had a CD player fitted in the boot** a few months ago. It takes six CDs at a time. So you get your favourite CDs, put it on random, and off you go. The good thing about random is you don't know which CD or which track you're going to hear next. **You get to listen to different kinds of music without having to stop or take your hands off the wheel.** And you can have the volume turned up as high as you like. It's brilliant on long journeys.

6

Woman **It's very strange, you just have to hear a certain sound or catch a whiff of a particular smell and everything comes flooding back.** I mean, I can remember exactly where I was when I heard Madonna's first hit. It was a winter evening. I was in my mother's kitchen and making myself a cheese sandwich. I only have to hear that first guitar chord and I'm back in my mum's kitchen. Another example is the smell of sun-tan lotion. It always takes me straight back to a holiday in Spain when I was four years old.

7

Man It's something I've always been terrified of, but it was absolutely killing me. In the end it got so bad, I just had to have it seen to. **Actually, it only needed filling,** which wasn't as bad as having to have it taken out. **Anyway I was sitting there in the chair, feeling very nervous, waiting for the drill,** when this wonderful Indian music started playing. It was incredible – my anxiety completely disappeared and I relaxed my whole body.

8

Woman **We now use music to help them recover – especially if they're here for a long stay.** Experimenting with different kinds of music, we've found that certain sounds have the power to change moods and emotional states for the better. Many of them come to us shattered, angry and full of pain, both physical and mental. They've had their lives reduced to a bed and a locker. We try to bring peace to their body and their mind.

Writing p98

Formal letter

1 Key

a The main purpose is to get a written explanation or a full refund of the membership fee.

b The letter should include the specific examples of how the leisure centre disappointed the member.

c The style should be formal.

2 Key

All of the information has been included. The style is too informal, specifically the phrases *pretty impressive, didn't have a clue, I am furious.* The style is also very aggressive, especially in the final paragraph.

3 Possible answer

Dear Sir,

I am writing to complain about Centre 2K, which I visited yesterday. I became a member *two weeks ago* after seeing your publicity, which was *very* impressive.

First, I went for a workout in the gym and found that two of your machines *were* out of order. I thought a member of staff might be able to help, but it took me ten minutes to find someone. *Despite being friendly*, he *did not know anything* about the machines.

Next, I went swimming. Unfortunately, the water *was not* heated, even though it was a cold evening.

Finally, I went to the café for a hot drink. However, when I got there it was closed, although it was only 10.45.

I am *very disappointed.* I *would like* a full written explanation *or I will* cancel my membership and request *a refund.*

Yours faithfully

Contrasting language

4 Key

Paragraph 2: but, despite
Paragraph 3: even though
Paragraph 4: However, although

5 Key

However

6 Key

a Although/Even though
b However
c even though
d but
e even though/although
f Despite

7 Possible answers

a Even though I take regular exercise, *I am still overweight.*
b I enjoy watching sport on TV, but *I don't like taking exercise.*
c Despite the fact that she couldn't drive, *Sue bought a car with her first salary.*
d I've never been to Australia. However, *I'd love to go.*
e Although I learnt to swim when I was quite young, *I get scared when I go in the sea.*

Think, plan, write

8 After students have read the task, ask the following questions: *What type of class have you enrolled on?* (swimming) *What are you unhappy about?* (the class began ten minutes late on two occasions; the instructors should be experienced but they were unable to answer some questions; the life-saving option that was offered wasn't available last week; there were not supposed to be others in the pool but there were children there last week)

10 Before they begin to write, encourage students to refer to the Writing guide on page 162.

Overview

1

1 unless I am doing
2 will be given instructions
3 are having our car serviced
4 all over the
5 not worth worrying about
6 were out of order
7 took five minutes to
8 came across

2 Key

a ex-wife	d midday
b post-dated	e anti-freeze
c semicircle	f undercharged

An extra activity to accompany this unit and a unit test can be downloaded from the Internet at www.oup.com/elt/teacher/exams

8 Media

Introduction p101

1 Possible answer

Picture 1: TV news is one of the most popular and effective ways of communicating information, although 24-hour news channels are very repetitive.

Picture 2: newspapers are a popular way of communicating information, but they are often politically biased. Also, the Internet is taking over.

Picture 3: despite more modern technology, radio is still a popular communication medium, especially digital radio or radio broadcasts on the Internet.

Picture 4: mobile phones are popular communication devices for personal messages, but they increasingly offer access to the Internet and TV.

Picture 5: computers offer access to all kinds of media – email, Internet, radio, TV, etc. Wi-fi connections and Internet telephone services make computers one of the most effective forms of communication.

2 Background information

Malcolm X was a prominent black nationalist leader in the USA. He was assassinated in 1965.

Jello Biafra is a punk musician and political activist from San Francisco.

WH Auden was a prominent Anglo-American poet. He died in 1973.

Listening p102

Lead in

1 Possible answers

You can exchange ideas with people of similar interests in a *chat room*.
You can *download* programs or music, such as *MP3* files.
You can play *online* games.
You can use a *search engine* to find *websites* that interest you, or you can *surf* the Net just by following the links.

Multiple matching

2 Make sure students read and think about the options before they listen to the recording.

Key

Speaker 1	B	Speaker 4	D
Speaker 2	E	Speaker 5	F
Speaker 3	A		
Extra letter: C		

Audioscript

Speaker 1   My friends all said it was really easy to use, but it took me ages to get the hang of the Internet. I suppose the more you use it the quicker you get. For me, it's a very environmentally-friendly thing. **I use it mainly for up-to-date news or reference**, so instead of getting into my car and driving down to the library, I just try my favourite search engine. I'd say in 99% of cases I find what I'm looking for in less time than it would take me to find what I'm looking for in books. And I've stopped getting a daily paper.

Speaker 2   Chat rooms – I'm addicted to them. I can't believe how easy it is to talk to people. **It's how I keep in touch with my friends and family**. At the moment I'm having regular chats with my older brother who's in Thailand. It's almost as good as the phone and so much cheaper. I've got into a few chats with people I don't know, but I haven't made any new friends though. I think it's a bit scary – the idea that you can get to know someone in a chat room. You don't really know anything about people – I mean, everything they tell you could easily be lies.

Speaker 3 I use it for various things – you know, the obvious ones – getting information, news, shopping. **But the best thing so far is tracking down people I was at school with.** There are quite a few sites now, where you can get in touch with people. It's amazing: **I've already found three people who were in the same class as me at primary school.** I've even met one of them who still lives quite near here. And I'm in email contact with someone I was at university with. She lives in the States now. I said I'd go and visit her next year if I could. It's fantastic!

Speaker 4 Music, definitely. It has to be music. That's about all I use it for really, apart from occasionally checking the sports results. It's fantastic if you're into modern music of any kind. I go on some of the music sites and download all kinds of MP3 files. Some of it's a bit weird. **If you've got your own CD burner you can make top quality CDs for next to nothing.** The music industry's trying to crack down on the illegal copying. They say they're losing sales because people like me aren't buying as many CDs. I reckon they're fighting a losing battle. **The thing is, apart from being free, it's amazingly quick.**

Speaker 5 I have to admit I fell in love with the Internet the first time I used it. I'd heard this incredible CD on the radio and I had to have it. **Most of the music shops in town said they'd never even heard of the band.** I phoned a specialist shop in London and asked if they had it in stock, but they said it was only available as an import. That's when I tried the Internet. I looked up the name of the band and found a list of their recordings. I put the CD I wanted into my basket, typed in my address and credit card number, and three days later it arrived by post. Magic!

Grammar and practice p103

Reporting statements

1 Key

  a It is really easy to use.
  b We've never even heard of the band.
  c I'll go and visit her next year if I can.
  d We're losing sales because people like you aren't buying as many CDs.

2 Key

  a The tense is generally moved one step back in time.
  b The reporting verb is in the present. Consequently, the other tenses have not changed. This implies that the situation is true in the present.

3 Key

  a He said (that) he'd stopped getting a daily newspaper.
  b She said (that) she was having regular chats with her older brother who was in Thailand.
  c She said (that) she had even met one of them who still lived quite near there.

Encourage students to refer to the Grammar reference on page 184.

Reporting questions

4 Key

The word order changes so that the subject comes before the verb just like in an affirmative sentence (*Have you got* becomes *if they had*; *When did they order* becomes *when they had ordered*). It is often necessary to change pronouns to the third person form (*he, she, it* and *they*).

5 Key

We use *if* in reported closed questions. *If* can be replaced by *whether*.

6 Key

  a The girl asked him if/whether he was on email.
  b Val asked Rob if/whether he used the Internet.
  c Nick asked me how long I had been interested in jazz.
  d Rachel asked Sharon which of her old school friends she had contacted.
  e Julie asked Tim if/whether he would like to contact people he was at school with.

Encourage students to refer to the Grammar reference on page 185.

Time references

7 Key

Sentence b can only be used if it is the same day as the original statement was made.

8 Encourage students to refer to the Grammar reference on page 185.

Key

last week – the week before
next month – the following month/the next month
next week – the following week/the next week
three days ago – three days before/three days earlier
today – that day
tomorrow – the next day/the following day
yesterday – the day before/the previous day

Other references

9 Key

The determiner *this* changes to *the*.
The place reference *here* changes to *there*.

10 Key

a Marsha asked Mr Hunt if the work had to be finished that day.
b Mr Gilbert asked if/whether there had been any phone calls for him the day before.
c The police officer informed Ian that the car had been stolen two weeks before.
d Dorothy said (that) she had written to her the week before and had phoned that morning.
e Matthew said that he had arranged to meet them after lunch the next day.

Reporting functions

11 Key

1 In sentence a, after *told Bob* there is a complete clause *She was leaving the next day*, which is a reported statement. In sentence b, after *told Bob* there is an infinitive structure *to leave her alone*, which is a reported command.
2 In sentence c, after *asked Bob* there is a complete clause *why he had done it*, which is a reported question. In sentence b, after *asked Bob* there is an infinitive structure *to leave his keys*, which is a reported request.
3 The infinitive is used.
4 The gerund (g) or a complete clause (h) can be used after *suggest*.

Encourage students to refer to the Grammar reference on page 186.

12 Key

a I'm leaving tomorrow.
b Leave me alone!
c Why did you do it?
d Could you leave your keys?
e Don't try and get in touch.
f You should try and forget her.
g Why don't we talk it over?
h Let's leave./You could leave/Why don't we leave?

Key word transformations

13 Key

1 warned us not to swim
2 advised Pete against buying/advised Pete not to buy
3 told Claire to take
4 asked John if/whether he could
5 offered to pick Tracy up
6 said he would see

Speaking p105

Long turn

3 Ask students to read the task. Then ask the following questions to check understanding. *What does Student A have to do first?* (compare the first two adverts) *What does Student A have to do after that?* (say which advert is likely to attract more attention) *How long should Student A talk for?* (about one minute) *What does Student B do when Student A has finished speaking?* (give an opinion about adverts on television)

Ask students to read the tip box, then ask *Why is it important to listen to what your partner is saying?* (You will have to make your own comments about the same subject.)

Monitor students as they do the task and give feedback to the class. (Did Student A complete both parts of the task? Did Student B listen properly? Did Student B give their opinion clearly?)

Possible answer

Both advertisements 1 and 2 show ways of getting people's attention through advertising. However, the advertisement using the steaming coffee is much more unusual than the decorated taxi. Advertising on taxis is a familiar sight, which may not get people's attention very easily. Consequently, the more unusual type of advertisement is much more likely to attract attention.

4 Repeat the procedure you followed for task 3.

Possible answers

Advertisements 3 and 4 both involve technology to get their message across. One is a TV ad, whereas the other is an Internet pop-up. The TV ad is more likely to reach a lot of people, but, of the other hand, the unusual pop-up may target customers more effectively. The main purpose of advertising like this is to give information about the products and influence consumers to identify a brand.

Over to you

Possible answers

Advertisement 1 is appealing to people who see this in the street. It uses a tactic based on surprising people. It is likely to appeal to people who appreciate its creativity.

Advertisement 2 is like a moving sign. It puts the idea of the product into people's minds. It is intended to reach anybody in a city environment.

Advertisement 3 is a TV ad, and it is appealing to anyone who enjoys watching moving rather than static images.

Advertisement 4, the Internet pop-up, seems aimed at people who are curious. Since some people may close it immediately, it needs to grab people's attention so that they activate the pop-up video.

Vocabulary p106

Compound nouns

1 Key

two or more nouns: bookcase, credit card, lunch-time, music shop
verb + preposition: breakdown, checkout,
preposition + verb: input

2 Key

two or more nouns: news editor, crime rate, community service, participation rate
verb + preposition: break-ins, clean-up

3 Key

computer programmer
news reader
shop assistant
television reporter
university lecturer

4 Key

disk drive   search engine
keyboard   website
mouse mat

5 Key

a make-up   d bypass
b outbreak   e breakdown/break-up
c take off

Optional activity

Give students the following definitions and ask them to identify the compound nouns.

1 It helps you find sites on the Internet.
2 You use this to give colour to your face.
3 It's where you pay for your goods in a supermarket.
4 It's the part of the computer that you type on.
5 It's a road that goes round a town.
6 It's what happens when something stops working.

(Answers: 1 search engine; 2 make-up; 3 checkout; 4 keyboard; 5 bypass; 6 breakdown)\

6 Key

keypad
mailbox
phonebook
ringtone
screensaver
text message

Word formation

7 Before they do the task, ask students to read the text and predict the kind of word they need to form to fill each of the gaps. (1 noun, 2 plural noun, 3 adverb, 4 adjective, 5 adjective, 6 plural noun, 7 plural noun, 8 adverb, 9 adjective, 10 adjective)

Key

1 retirement	6 meetings
2 rioters	7 elections
3 Certainly	8 properly
4 pleasant	9 dangerous
5 personal	10 predictable

Reading

2 Before they read, check students understand the meaning of the following phrases: *distractions* (something that takes your attention away from what you're doing), *strolling* (walking in a slow relaxed way), *dangling* (hanging or swinging freely), *chit-chat* (conversation about things that are not important).

Key

1 G	4 A	6 D
2 C	5 B	7 E
3 H		

Extra sentence: F

So and *such*

3 Key

Both are used for emphasis but *so* is used before an adjective or adverb and *such* is used before a noun (or a noun with an adjective before it).

4 Key

such: a lot of people, hot weather, little insects, tall trees
so: few cars, little time, many people, much money

5 Key

a so	c so	e Such
b such	d so	

Writing p110

Discursive essay

1 Key

a A discursive essay should start with an introduction and finish with a conclusion.
b by giving both sides of the argument
c A formal and impersonal style is best, although the conclusion may express a more personal view.

2 Key

a Paragraph 1: introduction
Paragraph 2: the opinions of famous people as understood by the writer
Paragraph 3: the opinion of newspapers as understood by the writer
Paragraph 4: the writer's opinion and conclusion
b The second paragraph describes how the relationship between a person and the media changes the more famous they become. The third paragraph describes the argument newspapers give for printing information about a famous person's private life.
c The writer's opinions are expressed in the last paragraph.
d Yes. The argument is presented impersonally and is structured appropriately.

Optional activity

To help students understand the meaning of the words in task 3, give them the following gapped information and ask them to use the words to complete the rules.

1 _____ and _____ are used to contrast two statements.
2 _____ introduces one side of the argument. _____ introduces the other side of the argument.
3 _____ means *actually* or *really*. It can be used to disprove an argument.
4 When you want to add a sentence that contrasts with the previous one, or gives another point of view you can use _____ .
5 _____ is used to give a conclusion.

(Answers: 1 although/whereas, 2 On the one hand/ On the other hand, 3 In fact, 4 however, 5 On balance)

Connecting ideas

3 Key

1 although/whereas
2 On the one hand
3 however
4 In fact
5 On the other hand
6 On balance
7 although

4 Key

a as well as (that), what is more, furthermore, apart from that, besides (this)
b nevertheless, on the contrary, by contrast
c in conclusion, in short, on the whole, to conclude, to summarise, to sum up

5 Key

they – the newspapers
these different points of view – the views of newspapers and famous people
they – the famous people
their – the famous people
they – the newspapers
this – the writer's opinion that stars deserve some privacy

8 Possible answers

In favour of a ban

It's morally wrong to advertise something that can damage your health.
Advertising often makes dangerous products seem glamorous to young people.
People are not always fully informed about the bad effects of smoking/drinking.

Against a ban

A ban would be against freedom of speech/ideas.
People should be allowed to make up their own minds.
Enough warnings are already given on cigarette packets.

Encourage students to refer to the Writing guide on page 167.

Overview p112

1 Key

1 competition	6 criminals
2 fully	7 registration
3 convenience	8 visiting
4 addition	9 easily
5 attractive	10 identification

2 Key

Jayne said she was going on holiday the next day.
Ben asked (her) if she was going anywhere special.
Jayne replied that she was, Australia. She said that she would be staying in Perth for a week and then going on to Sydney.
Ben asked (her) who she was going with.
Jayne replied that she was going with two of her friends from work.

3 Key

a I've always wanted to go to Australia.
b Would you like to come with us?
c I certainly would.
d I'll see if there are any places left on the flight.
e I'm not sure if I can afford it.
f I'll lend you the money.

4 Key

a so	c such	e so
b so	d such	

An extra activity to accompany this unit, a unit test and Progress Test 2 (Units 5–8) can be downloaded from the Internet at www.oup.com/elt/teacher/exams

9 Around us

Introduction p113

1 Possible answers

a Extreme heat can make it difficult for people to work or sleep. It can create an increased danger of skin problems and some infectious diseases.
Extreme cold can cause hypothermia. Travelling can be hazardous. Some machines cannot work at low temperatures.

2 Possible answers

a Flooding would probably affect more people because more people have their homes near rivers than in or near forests.

b Forest fires can be avoided by increasing restrictions on what people can do in dry areas, such as lighting camp fires but sometimes the fires can be started by lightning, which is unavoidable. People can avoid the problems by building homes well away from woodland.
Flooding can be avoided by controlling water flow in rivers and by carefully planning building and its effects on the environment.

Reading p114

Think ahead

1 Key

a 3   b 3   c 2

Multiple choice

3 You may like to check students understand the following words in the text: *molten* (burning), *earth's core* (central part of the earth), *growth* (increase), *potential* (what's possible), *imprecise* (inexact), *evacuating* (leaving a place to escape danger), *hazard zones* (dangerous places),

monitoring (observing, checking), *detect* (find), *evaluating* (understanding, assessing), *plumes* (clouds, columns), *loss of credibility* (when something is no longer believed), *proximity* (surrounding area).

Ask students to work out the answer to the first question (D). Then ask why the other options are incorrect. (A Wealthy women are mentioned, but we are told they died. Nobody escaped. B Only two towns – *Herculaneum* and *Pompeii* are mentioned. C 16,000 people died. This is definitely not a few.) When students have completed the remaining questions, ask them to justify their answers in the same way.

Key

1 D	4 A	6 B
2 C	5 C	7 A
3 C		

Over to you

Possible answers

People often choose to live near volcanoes because the agricultural land is very fertile. It would be difficult to evacuate a large city because people might panic, the transport network could get congested, and emergency accomodation would be required. The best solution would be to practise and make full use of emergency services.

Word-building

4 Key

compete – competition
erupt – eruption
evacuate – evacuation
fascinate – fascination
populate – population
migrate – migration
They are all formed with the suffix *-tion*.

5 Key

act – active
danger – dangerous
destroy – destruction
science – scientific
system – systematic
volcano – volcanic

6 Key

a scientific   e fascination
b dangerous   f population
c migration   g active
d systematic   h competition

Grammar and practice p116

Relative clauses

1 Key

a which, which/that
b who/that

2 Key

The speaker has more than one sister in
sentence a. In sentence a, the information in the
relative clause is essential.
The speaker has only one sister in sentence b. In
sentence b, the information in the relative clause
is not essential.

3 Key

a defining
b non-defining – …, who study volcanic
  activity, …
c non-defining – …, which is the hot molten
  rock emitted from a volcano when it
  erupts, …
d non-defining – …, which can be carried on
  the wind for thousands of kilometres.
e defining
f defining

4 Encourage students to refer to the Grammar
reference on page 186.

Key

In sentences a and e, *which* can be replaced with
that.

5 Key

a where   b , when   c why
The relative pronoun can be left out of
sentence c.

6 Encourage students to refer to the Grammar
reference on page 187.

Key

The sentences with *whom* are more formal than
the sentences with *who*. You use *whom*, not *who*,
immediately after a preposition.

7 Key

a who/that
b which/that
c why/—
d , which
e which/that
f where
g , whose latest film was shot in LA,
h whose
i that/which/—
j , when

Cloze

8 Check students understand the text by asking the
following questions: *What did the native
Americans originally hunt?* (buffalo) *How did the
first white settlers survive?* (they had cattle) *What
negative effects did the crop-growing farmers have
on the land?* (they dug up the grass to plant crops
which meant the soil wasn't anchored and easily
blew away during droughts) *Where did the farmer
decide to go?* (California) *How did the government
help the farmers who had remained?* (it gave them
money) *What was the money for?* (to change the
land back to grassland)

Remind students to use the words on either side
of the gaps to help them decide what kind of
words are missing.

Key

1 where   7 their
2 on   8 of
3 was   9 Finally / Reluctantly / Eventually
4 other   10 who
5 no   11 spite
6 which   12 so

Ask students to read the text and find words that
have the following meanings: wandered about
(*roamed*), allowed something to continue
(*sustained*), environment, plant life, etc.
(*ecology*), long periods of time when there's no
rain (*droughts*), kept in one place (*anchored*),
people moving from one place to another
(*migrants*), payment as a form of help (*subsidy*),
changed back again (*converted*).

Vocabulary p118

3 Ask students how the weather is changing according to the article (temperatures are rising).

Key

The article says that greenhouse gas emissions and tropical deforestation are to blame for climate changes.

Dependent prepositions

4 Key

consequences *for*
responsible *for*
leads *to*

5 Key

agreement on	effect on
anger at	respect for
ban on	tax on
cure for	threat to
damage to	

a cure for   c respect for
b threat to   d tax on

6 Key

a to, to   b of, to   c of, to, for   d for

7 Key

appeal to	insist on
believe in	invest in
complain about	sympathise with
contribute to	result in
depend on	

8 Key

a 3 on   b 5 to   c 1 in   d 2 about   e 4 with

Optional activity

1 Ask students to match the following words from the vocabulary page with these prepositions.

in   on   to   for   of

1 capable	5 ban
2 invest	6 opposed
3 threat	7 contribute
4 respect	8 believe

(Answers: 1 of, 2 in, 3 to, 4 for, 5 on, 6 to, 7 to, 8 in)

2 Ask students to use the words in their own sentences.

Key word transformations

9 Key

a a ban on cars
b makes a contribution towards
c do not (don't) sympathise with
d to make an investment in
e be incapable of changing
f result in a saving of
g have a negative effect on
h is anger at

Speaking p120

Lead in

1 Possible answers

Students might refer to the photos for ideas: driving cars or using other forms of transport which burn fuels, throwing away rubbish, using detergents, burning things which give off smoke or fumes, overfishing.

Other ideas include: using unnecessary wrapping for products or containers made of plastic, cutting down trees, using pesticides, polluting rivers and seas, building roads through countryside, nuclear power plants and growing genetically-modified foods.

Two-way task

3 Establish what is happening in the photos and write a list of key vocabulary on the board. (For example: exhaust fumes, pollution, recycling; noise pollution; energy; harmful chemicals; smoke; harmful gases; fish stocks, etc.) This will help students in the speaking task.

After students have read the task, ask the following questions to check they know what they have to do: *What should you talk about first?* (how each of the activities in the photos affects the environment) *What should you do second?* (agree on two activities that it would be easy to stop doing)

While students are doing the task, monitor their discussions and give feedback to the class about their performance at the end. (Did they complete both parts of the task effectively? Did they listen to each other and speak for equal amounts of time?)

Possible answers

Using motor vehicles produces chemicals which make the streets unhealthy, and contributes to global warming through the production of greenhouse gases.

Throwing away unnecessary litter, such as excess packaging, can make the streets dirty and fills up rubbish dumps with material which is not biodegradable.

Air travel causes noise pollution for those who live near airports and also produces large amounts of greenhouse gases.

Using household appliances such as washing mashines uses up electricity which may be generated by burning fossil fuels. Also, some detergents are damaging to the environment.

Burning household and garden waste can generate bad smells and contributes to the greenhouse effect.

Buying and eating certain species of fish can have a damaging effect on the marine environment. In particular, some species of fish, like cod, are now heavily overfished and populations may not recover..

Discussion

4 Students can do this task in pairs. Monitor their discussions and give feedback to the class about their performance. (Did they give good reasons for their opinions? Did they encourage each other to speak?)

Listening p121

Think ahead

2 Possible answers

Air travel releases carbon dioxide into the atmosphere which can contribute to global warming. The situation could be improved by technical adjustments to aeroplanes or aeroplane fuels. Otherwise, people could take fewer flights. This could be encouraged by taxing air travel more heavily.

Multiple choice

3 Audioscript

Presenter Welcome to our weekly topical discussion programme 'In the news'. This week and over the next few weeks we shall be looking at climate change and in particular what we as individuals can do to reverse the current trend. You will all by now have heard the term 'carbon footprint'. By 'carbon footprint' we mean a measure of the impact that human activities have on the environment in terms of the amount of greenhouse gases they produce. These days it is easy to work out how big one's own personal carbon footprint is – provided you've got Internet access. **You can simply go online, put the following information in – how much your annual household fuel bill is; how, how often and how far you travel – and a calculator will work it out for you. That gives you your primary carbon footprint.** Your secondary carbon footprint is determined by your buying habits. Basically, if you buy food or items produced locally then your carbon footprint will be smaller than if you buy produce which has to be either flown or shipped in from the other side of the world. **There are of course ways of reducing the size of our carbon footprint: we can car share to work, travel by bus or train rather than by car, and use the train or coach instead of taking domestic flights.** We can buy local fruit or veg and buy local wine – if you live in the UK then buy from European countries rather than Australia, South Africa or South America. And we should try to buy clothes or products from closer to home and avoid items that have been made in China or India, for example. Another thing we can do is offset our carbon footprint. We can do this by planting trees as these breathe in carbon dioxide and produce oxygen, thus reducing the amount and percentage of CO_2 in the atmosphere. In today's programme we shall be discussing the effect of air travel on the environment. Suzanne Hendry, you're a marketing director from Edinburgh. How have you been addressing this?

Suzanne Hendry Thank you. I quit flying a year ago because I realised that all my other efforts to be green – recycling, exchanging my gas-guzzling 4x4 for an electric car, and insulating my house would be wiped out by a couple of holidays by air. For too long I had been saying 'they', i.e. governments, must do something about global warming rather than 'we' or 'I' and **I suddenly realised that I can't expect things to change if I'm not prepared to change myself.** How would I be able to look my own five-year-old daughter in the eye in twenty years' time and say 'I could have done something but I chose not to'?

Presenter   What convinced you to take that step?

Suzanne Hendry   The arguments against flying are obvious. **Do you know that one return flight London–Florida produces the equivalent carbon dioxide to a year's motoring? A return flight to Australia equals the emissions of three average cars for a year?** And if you fly from London to Edinburgh for the weekend you produce eight times the carbon dioxide you would use if you took the train? Also because the pollution is released at altitude its effect on climate change is more than double that on the ground.

Presenter   Nigel Hammond? You're in the travel industry. What's the present situation?

Nigel Hammond   There has been a huge rise in the number of people flying. Do you know that in 1970 British airports were used by 32 million people; in 2004 the figure was 216 million and in 2030, according to government forecasts, the figure will be around 500 million! The cheap flights offered by budget airlines have meant that more and more people think nothing of popping over to the continent for the weekend. Long-haul destinations are becoming increasingly popular too, even though ticket prices haven't seen the same reductions. **But the biggest rise has been in short-haul flights both domestic and to places like Spain, France, and Italy.**

Suzanne Hendry   I think the problem is that although most people know that flying contributes hugely to global warming they are not really prepared to do anything about it. **So they'll feel a bit bad while they're sitting on the plane flying to wherever it is they're going but the moment they get to their destination it'll be long forgotten.** It certainly won't stop them planning their next weekend trip on their return.

Presenter   I think that's very true. So what solutions are there? Are there any?

Nigel Hammond   There are a variety of solutions on offer. One is to put up the tax on aviation fuel. This has been tried already and didn't work and I'm not really sure that an increase in tax is the best idea anyway. A lot of people are against it because they say it's a tax on the poor. **Another is to**

limit the number of flights that people can take a year. I like that idea but I'm not sure how practical it would be. Still I think it would be worth giving it a go. And then of course there is carbon offsetting whereby people plant trees on the other side of the world. The problem with that is that if they're cut down or there's a fire you've lost your offset. At the end of the day, ...

4   Make sure students read the questions before they listen to the recording for a second time.

Key

1 C	4 A	6 C
2 B	5 A	7 B
3 B		

Writing p122

Informal email

1   Check students have understood by asking the following questions about the advert: *Where is the holiday?* (Nepal) *How long is it for?* (fourteen or twenty-one days) *What kind of holiday is it?* (developing projects to help tourism in the local area) *Where can you stay?* (with local families) *What can you do at the end of the holiday?* (go trekking) *What extra costs are there?* (food and drink on days off)

Key

a   Dear/Hi, Yours/Love/Best wishes
b   The email should be written in an informal style.

Asking for information

2   Key

How long do you want to go for?
What other projects do they offer?
Can you choose which projects to do?
How basic are the facilities?
Is there a toilet?
How much will the food and drink cost?

3   Possible answers

Could you tell me how long you want to go for?
Can you find out what other projects they offer?
Do you know if we can choose which projects to do?
Could you find out how basic the facilities are?
Do you know if there is a toilet?
Could you find out how much food and drink costs?

4 Possible answers

   1 You didn't say when you wanted to go.

   2 How long do you want to go for?

   3 How much does it cost?

   4 Can you find out what other projects they offer

   5 Could you also find out how basic the facilities are?

5 Possible answers

   a Where exactly is Kankali village?
     Do you know where exactly Kankali village is?

   b How far is it from the airport?
     Could you find out how far it is from the airport?

   c Are there holidays like this all year round?
     Could you tell me if there are holidays like this all year round?

   d What sort of clothes should I bring?
     Could you find out what sort of clothes I should bring?

   e How long can you stay in Nepal at the end of the holiday?
     I'd like to know how long you can stay in Nepal at the end of the holiday.

Think, plan, write

6 After students have read the task and the information, check they have understood by asking the following questions: *Who have you received an email from?* (your friend, Sam) *Who are you going to write to?* (Maria) *Who is Maria?* (Somebody you have both met) *What do you want to know about?* (a holiday in Nepal) *Which village did Maria go to?* (Kankali) *What information does Sam want to know?* (the age of volunteers; whether you need to be a good walker) *What information do you want to know?* (food; clothes; whether it's worth going)

7 Encourage students to refer to the Writing guide on page 164.

Overview p124

1 Key

   1 , which is situated near the Bay of Naples,

   2 , who believed it to be extinct,

   3 which/that

   4 , which happened when no one was expecting it,

   5 , when

   6 who

   7 whose

2 Key

   1 is not safe to swim

   2 search for clues was done

   3 despite being ninety

   4 his fascination with

   5 great deal of

3 Key

a in	c to	e to
b at	d of, of	f on

An extra activity to accompany this unit and a unit test can be downloaded from the Internet at www.oup.com/elt/teacher/exams

10 Innovation

Introduction p125

1 Possible answers

1 A CD, which was originally intended for recording music or computer data, is being used as a drinks coaster.
2 Cola cans, which were originally used as containers for soft drinks, have been used as a material to make toy cars.
3 A rubber tyre, which was originally intended for car wheels, is being used as a swing for children.
4 Empty containers, which were probably used for cooking oil, are being used as watering cans.
5 A coat hanger, which was originally used to hang up clothes, is being used as a car aerial.
6 Two empty tins, which were originally used as containers for food, are being used as a toy telephone.

3 Possible answers

1 A barrel could be used as a container for food waste for reycling as compost, or could be used as a bin for other substances.
2 A paper clip could be used as a bookmark, or as a way of keeping money together.
3 An old tin could be used to store coins or jewellery or as a container to keep matches dry on a camping trip.
4 A blanket could be used for sitting on in the garden or in the park, or it could be used as a wall hanging. It could be used as a canopy or a sunshade if it were hung over branches or secured by sticks.
5 A brick could be used as a doorstop, a bookend or as an ashtray.
6 An empty drinks bottle could be cut into different shapes and be turned into a funnel or a plant pot. It could be used by young children to create models and for collecting and measuring rainwater for geography projects.

Reading p126

Lead in

2 Key

A 4   B 3   C 2   D 1

Multiple matching

3 Key

1	C	8	B
2	D	9	C
3	A	10, 11	A, C
4, 5	B, D	12	D
6	A	13, 14	B, D
7	C	15	B

Grammar and practice p128

Wishes and regrets

1 Key

a past situation
b present or future situation
c present or future situation

A wish about a present or future situation is expressed with a past tense. A wish about a past situation is expressed with a past perfect tense.

2 Key

Would or *wouldn't* are used after *wish* to complain about a present situation.

3 Key

Sentence b with *if only* expresses the stronger regret.

4 Possible answers

Some suggestions are given in the cartoons at the foot of this page.

5 Key

1 could afford to go
2 wish you would clean
3 he had remembered to send
4 had gone to bed earlier
5 she was/were as tall as
6 only I had not told

I'd rather and *It's time ...*

6 Key

a When the speaker expresses their own preference, they use the infinitive without *to* immediately after the expression *I'd rather*.
b When the speaker expresses a preference about somebody or something else, they use a pronoun, name or thing after the expression *I'd rather* and the past form of the verb.

7 Key

Sentence a is more urgent.
a past tense
b infinitive

Encourage students to refer to the Grammar reference on page 188.

8 Key

a to go
b met
c got/had
d told, know
e took
f do, did
g tidied

Cloze

9 Ask students to read through the text before they begin the task. Ask the following question: *In what way was the invention of Post-it notes an accident?* (The person who invented the weak glue that is used on Post-its was originally trying to invent a very strong glue.)

Key

1 until
2 across
3 all
4 of
5 had
6 what / one
7 could
8 but
9 to
10 they
11 without
12 one

Speaking p130

Lead in

1 Background information

The first printing machine using moveable type was invented by a German man called Johannes Gutenberg in the fifteenth century. It was worked by hand. Before it was invented, most books were written by hand.

Cameras were invented in 1839. The first portable Kodak cameras were invented in 1889. Before cameras were invented, there was only painting and sculpture.

The telephone was introduced in 1876 by Alexander Graham Bell. Before it was invented, people used the telegram to send messages.

The first light bulb was made in 1879 by Thomas Edison. Before it was invented, people used candles and fuel lamps for light.

The modern motor vehicle was invented by Karl Benz in 1893. Before this, the most common forms of land transportation were by foot, by horse, or by train.

Two-way task

2 After students have read the task, ask the following questions: *What do you have to do first?* (talk together about each of the breakthroughs shown in the photos) *What do you have to do after that?* (decide together on two breakthroughs which you would include in an article on historical breakthroughs)

While students are doing the task, monitor their discussions and give feedback to the class about their performance. (Did they complete both tasks effectively? Did they listen and respond to each other's comments and suggestions?)

Possible answers

Printing has affected the way we live by enabling easier distribution of and access to information in the form of books, magazines and newspapers.

Photography has allowed images of our lives to be recorded. It has also influenced entertainment in the form of film.

Telecommunication has influenced how we communicate with friends and family, as well as allowing technology such as the Internet.

As well as lighting our homes, *electricity* has enabled us to use labour-saving devices such as washing machines and microwave ovens.

Breakthroughs in *travel* have made the world a smaller place. The motor car and the aeroplane have enabled people to travel more often and further, both for work and for leisure.

Vocabulary p131

Lead in

1 Key

Products and inventions are named after the inventor, after a description of what they do, by combining sounds or words, or by using initials or acronyms.

Adjective suffixes

3 Key

Descriptive is related to *describe*. (suffix: *-ive*)
Mechanical is related to *mechanic*. (suffix: *-al*)
Careful is related to *care*. (suffix: *-ful*)
Disastrous is related to *disaster*. (suffix: *-ous*)
Speedy is related to *speed*. (suffix: *-y*)
Reliable is related to *rely*. (suffix: *-able*)

4 Key

a sticky
b useful, useless
c economic
d advisable
e fashionable, stretchy
f favourable
g creative, original
h protective, scientific, dangerous

5 Key

a agricultural, industrial
b political
c offensive
d homeless
e comfortable

Optional activity

1 Match the words to the definitions and add suitable suffixes to make adjectives.

danger   speed   industry   home   use   fashion
create   origin

1 Something that travels fast is _____
2 Something which is ineffective is _____
3 An _____ idea is something that nobody has thought of before.
4 A popular item of clothing is _____
5 People who sleep on the streets are _____
6 A _____ person is usually good at the arts.
7 Something that can cause harm is _____
8 A town full of factories is known as _____

(Answers: 1 speedy   2 useless   3 original
4 fashionable   5 homeless   6 creative
7 dangerous   8 industrial)

2 Students use the words to make their own sentences.

Listening p132

Think ahead

1 Key

1 This is an automatic drinks stirrer, allowing you to stir a drink by pressing a button with your thumb instead of using a spoon.
2 This is a mini paper-shredder for destroying confidential documents.
3 This is a voice-activated remote control for operating other electrical appliances.
4 This is a waterproof radio which can be used in a shower.
5 This is a fly trap which catches flying insects in your home.
6 This is an artificial cat which appears to breathe like a real one.

2 Possible answer

People sometimes buy gadgets because they are interested in technology or impressed by new inventions. Often gadgets are entertaining or unusual in some way.

Sentence completion

3 Key

He mentions the voice-activated remote control, the breathing cat and the fly-catcher.

Audioscript

Interviewer	Good afternoon. And this afternoon we're pleased, very pleased indeed, to welcome Paul Turner, self-confessed gadget freak and author of the book *Gadgets: Do we need them?*
Paul	Which is in all good bookshops now. Pleased to be here.
Interviewer	Paul, can I start off by asking you, is there a gap between the generations in their attitude towards gadgets?
Paul	Yes, definitely. I think people's attitudes towards gadgets are definitely a generation thing. My father, for example, who's in his 80s, has never really understood why gadgets **fascinate** me so much. It's just completely beyond his comprehension.
Interviewer	Is it because people of our generation have grown up with gadgets, do you think?
Paul	I think that's one of the reasons, yes, but the main one, in my opinion, is that people of our parent's generation have a completely different attitude to **money** from people of our generation, and from the younger generation even more so. My

father lived through the war, when times were hard, and he actually physically cringes every time he sees me spend money. What I see as a necessity, he sees as a luxury – something that is not an **essential** at all.

Interviewer   So how much of a gadget freak are you?

Paul   Well, my wife recently counted the number of **remote controls** we had in the house and it came to the grand total of thirty-eight. This one I use a lot. It's voice-activated. You speak into it like so and hey presto the TV or whatever switches on or off.

Interviewer   But isn't that the same as an ordinary remote?

Paul   Well, yes ... but that's not really the point.

Interviewer   So what does your wife think about all this?

Paul   She hates gadgets. She thinks I'm **obsessed**. And I am. I don't mind admitting it. We're always rowing about it. But I can't help it. I love them. In my view, anything that makes life easier or **more fun** is certainly worth having.

Interviewer   Do you use all the gadgets that you buy?

Paul   I have to admit that I don't, not all of them. Some are so high-tech that you can't work out how to use them. If I can't follow the instructions – often they're **not clear** – then I have been known to give up on them, yes.

Interviewer   What on earth's that? It looks like an old fur coat!

Paul   Ah, this one. It's just a bit of fun. Look you stroke it like this and it breathes and sort of purrs.

Interviewer   But a real cat does that.

Paul   Ah, yes but with this cat there's no expense, no mess. And no scratches on the furniture.

Interviewer   (laughs) Do you think gadgets are more of a male thing?

Paul   Mm I'm not sure about that. I know a lot of women who are just as gadget-mad as I am. But then again, I know some women who buy a lot of gadgets but never use them. My sister is a bit like that. When she gets a new gadget she's like a kid with a new toy. She uses it for a few weeks and then gets **bored**, so it ends up in a drawer somewhere.

Interviewer   I know a few people like that. Finally, I have to ask this. Does anybody really need all these gadgets?

Paul   Well to be honest, no.

Interviewer   So why do we buy them?

Paul   A lot of technology purchases are a case of keeping up with **other people**. If you don't have something and **other people** do, you feel you're missing out. That's why a lot of people buy things.

Interviewer   Do you have a favourite gadget?

Paul   Usually my favourite is my most recent purchase. This one I've got here is amazing. Let me show you how it works. You put it on your desk in the summer when there are lots of **flies** about, put some bait inside – you get a supply when you buy it – wait and when a fly flies past it's attracted to the bait, flies in, the plant snaps shut – one dead fly! It's daft but it's fun, don't you think?

4   After students have read through the gapped sentences, ask them to think about what kind of word might be missing. (a adjective, b noun, c adjective, d plural noun, e adjective, f comparative adjective, g adjective, h adjective, i noun, j noun)

Key

a fascinated
b money
c essential
d remote controls
e obsessed

f more fun
g not clear/unclear
h bored (with it)
i other people
j flies

Vocabulary p133

Lead in

1 Key

screen and teenager
Japan and animation
Frankenstein and food
iPod and broadcast
adult and adolescent

Compound adjectives

3 Key

a long-lasting
b big-eyed, round-faced
c world-famous

4 Possible answers

fat-free – milk, yoghurt, other food products
mass-produced – cars, toys
home-made – bread, biscuits, cakes
king-sized – bed
cold-blooded – reptiles, person
hard-wearing – shoes, other items of clothing
that last a long time

5 Key

a fast-flowing
b sugar-free
c fast-growing

d grey-haired
e good-looking

6 Key

a dark-skinned
b long-legged
c brown-eyed

d big-headed
e thick-skinned
f kind-hearted

Writing p134

Review

1 Key

King Kong (1933, Merian C Cooper and Ernest B Schoedsack) was a landmark horror/action film. It used animation to create many of the scenes involving dinosaurs and the giant gorilla Kong.

The Lord of the Rings trilogy (2001–2003, Peter Jackson), based on the famous trilogy of books by Tolkien,was innovative in its use of special effects to create fantasy creatures and their interaction with human actors. Much of the animation was digital.

Shrek 2 (2004, Andrew Adamson, Kelly Asbury, and Conrad Vernon) tells the story of the ogre Shrek and his wife Fiona. It is innovative in its complete use of computer animation to tell the story.

Other innovations include the early use of sound, early animation, and the use of digital movie cameras.

2 Possible answer

You should include a brief synopsis of the contents of the story, without giving away the end, and say whether you would or would not recommend it.

3 Possible answers

b The review is written in an informal, chatty style.
c Possible three stars.

Evaluative adjectives

4 Possible answers

Adjectives in the review
fake
first rate
overcomplicated
stunning

Positive
clever
entertaining
exciting
first rate
funny
hilarious
original
spectacular
stunning
witty
wonderful

Negative
amateurish
disappointing
dull
fake
over-complicated
over-long
predictable
tedious
unconvincing
wooden

5 Key

a predictable
b stunning / spectacular
c amateurish / unconvincing / wooden
d entertaining
e over-complicated

6 Possible answers

Plays	Musicals	Concerts	Ballet
act	act	conductor	choreography
cast	cast		costumes
costumes	choreography		lighting
lighting	costumes		
plot	lighting		
scene	scene		
scenery	scenery		

TV	Books	Music	Restaurants
cast	design	track	décor
commentary	plot		lighting
plot	series		presentation
scene			service
stunt			
series			
soundtrack			
special effects			

Think, plan, write

7 Encourage students to refer to the Writing Guide on page 168.

Overview p136

1 Key

1 controversial	6 latest
2 contribution	7 criticisms
3 choice	8 traditional
4 Exhibition	9 photographer
5 winner	10 argument

2 Key

a hadn't lost
b wouldn't interrupt
c could go
d had met
e didn't have, had
f had applied
g left
h got
i didn't bring
j told

3 Key

a carries me back
b carried on
c carry them through
d carried away
e carry out

An extra activity to accompany this unit and a unit test can be downloaded from the Internet at www.oup.com/elt/teacher/exams

11 Communication

Reading p138

Lead in

1 Possible answers

1 surprise	4 enjoyment
2 disgust	5 sadness
3 anger	6 fear

Gapped text

3 Before students read the text, you may want to check that they understand these words: *unique* (original, the only one), *classified* (categorised), *derive* (come from), *conceived* (first thought of), *contempt* (dislike).

Encourage students to justify their answers by finding reference words in the text.

Key

1 B	4 A	6 E
2 G	5 H	7 D
3 F		

Extra sentence: C

Grammar and practice p140

Conditionals 0, 1 and 2

1 Key

Type 0: present simple, present simple
Type 1: present simple, *will* + infinitive
Type 2: past simple, *would* + infinitive

2 Key

a Type 2   b Type 0   c Type 1

3 Key

a future possibility
b imaginary/impossible

4 Key

a If the situation arises (and this is likely to happen) the speaker in the first sentence is more sure of the desire to work abroad than the speaker in the second sentence.
b If the situation arises (and this is not very likely to happen) the speaker in the first sentence is more sure of the desire to work abroad than the speaker in the second sentence.

Encourage students to refer to the Grammar reference on page 189.

5 Make sure students use the correct structure for Type 0 conditional sentences:

If + present simple or imperative

Possible answers

b If I have good news to pass on, I *normally telephone all my friends.*
c If someone has upset me, I *buy myself something nice like a new CD.*
d If I need a friend's advice, I *talk to the people I trust most.*
e If I want to apologise for something I've done, I *sometimes buy a bunch of flowers.*

6 Possible answers

a If you watch too much television, *you become lazy.* (Type 0)
b If you don't go to bed earlier, *you'll be too tired to study.* (Type 1)
c I'll do the washing up if *you clean the kitchen.* (Type 1)
d If you lend me your car for the evening, *I'll take you out for a meal tomorrow.* (Type 1)
e If you don't work harder, *you'll fail your exams.* (Type 1)
f I'd spend more time at home if *I liked my flatmates.* (Type 2)

Conditional 3

7 Key

If you *had given* (past perfect) me your number, I *would have sent* (would + has/have + past participle) you a message.

8 Key

This type of conditional sentence is used to imagine different possible results for a situation in the past which cannot be changed.

Key word transformations

9 Key

1 had known it was you
2 if I had known
3 because she did not have
4 have been late if
5 if I had not forgotten
6 we would have come

10 Encourage students to refer to the Grammar reference on page 189.

Possible answer

If I had been Jill Frame, I wouldn't have crossed the motorway. If I had been her, I would have waved to passing motorists until one of them phoned the police.

Mixed conditionals

11 Key

The holiday has already happened in sentence a. They haven't gone on holiday yet in sentence b.

12 Possible answers

a If I hadn't learnt to read, *I wouldn't be at university.*
b If I'd won the lottery at the weekend, *I'd be in the Caribbean now!*
c If I'd saved all my money for the last year, *I'd be able to buy a new car.*
d If I hadn't had a good education, *I'd be earning less money today.*
e If I'd been born into a rich family, *I wouldn't have to work.*
f If my mother hadn't met my father, *I wouldn't be here.*

Encourage students to refer to the Grammar reference on page 190.

Unless, as long as, provided that

13 Key

a Unless you work harder, you'll fail your exams.
b You'll pass your driving test as long as you practise enough.
c You can borrow my car provided that you buy your own petrol.
d You can't telephone me unless you have some important news.

Encourage students to refer to the grammar reference on page 190.

14 Key

b I'll never speak to you again unless *you take back what you just said.*
c I'll lend you the money you need as long as *you pay me back next week.*

Listening p142

Multiple choice

3 Make sure students read through the questions and options before they listen to the recording.

Key

1 A	4 A	7 B
2 C	5 A	8 B
3 B	6 A	

Audioscript

1

Woman   I was at my boyfriend's house a couple of weeks ago, and his mother asked me if I'd like to stay for lunch. **I said I was expected home, but it was a complete lie** – I'd actually told my parents I'd be out all day and not to expect me home before the evening. The thing is, I'd eaten at his house before and the food was terrible. But you can't tell the truth in situations like that, can you?

2

Interviewer   So why do you think the general public don't trust people like you?

Man   I think there are two main reasons. Firstly, we're famous for breaking our promises, aren't we? **When we want people to vote for us, we pretend that we can make everything right.** We say things like 'This time next year you'll all have more money in your pocket'. And sometimes it's impossible to make these things happen – it's then that people accuse us of telling lies. The second reason is to do with the party system – we all have to say we agree with our party leader, whether we really do or not.

3

Woman I'm not really keen on lying, but I was in town the other day and I bumped into one of my neighbours. She said she'd heard that my sister and her husband had split up, and she wanted to know if it was true. I kept a straight face and said I'd no idea. It was a lie, of course – I mean I'd known about it for ages, but I wasn't going to give our family secrets away to someone I hardly knew. **The trouble is, she'd have wanted to know all the details, and everyone would have known by the weekend.**

4

Woman I have to admit, life would have been dull if I hadn't told the occasional lie. Not wicked ones – just little lies that don't hurt anyone. I remember once at a party, I got stuck with this really boring boy. All he could talk about was football. After about twenty minutes, I was really fed up, so I told him my cousin played for England – his eyes nearly popped out of his head. He wanted to know my cousin's name, and could I introduce him. When I said it was David Beckham, I thought he was going to faint with excitement. It's not true – **I just wanted to see his face.**

5

Man On the way back, I was really tired. I should have stopped for a quick nap, but I didn't. I kept going 'cos it was late and I wanted to get home. It was easy driving – there was hardly any traffic on the road. **But unfortunately, I nodded off for a second, went off the road and scraped the car against a tree.** There wasn't much damage to the car – and I was fine after that. As soon as I got home, I told my dad that I'd hit a tree, but what I didn't say was that I'd nodded off.

6

Woman The other day, the phone rang, and my brother asked me to answer it. He thought it was probably his friend Barbara and he didn't want to speak to her. He asked me to say he wasn't in. Actually, it wasn't Barbara – it was another friend of his: Annie. Anyway, I just said he was out. Later, when I told him who it was, he was absolutely furious. His exact words were: **'If I'd known it was Annie, I'd have spoken to her.'** That's one of the problems about lying for someone else, isn't it?

7

Woman Didn't you think it was a bit strange, someone offering you such a bargain at a motorway service area?

Man Not really. It looked exactly like the real thing. And anyway, I've needed a new one for ages – mine hasn't kept proper time since I dropped it in the bath.

Woman So when did you realise you'd been tricked?

Man **As soon as I took it out of its case, I knew it was a fake.** When I turned it over it said **Made in Toyland** on the back!

8

Woman My sister was on holiday last summer. She was expecting her exam results towards the end of August and she'd asked me to open her letters and telephone her with the results as soon as they arrived. She'd only been away about a week when the letter came – I was so excited, I just ripped it open without thinking. I couldn't believe it. She'd failed. I didn't know what to do. I couldn't tell her. She rang the next day and I said the letter hadn't come. **I mean, if I'd told her the result, it would have ruined her holiday.**

Collocations with *say, speak, talk* and *tell*

4 Key

a speak	d say	g talking
b tell	e told	h tell
c speak	f tell	

Confusing verbs: *hope, wait, expect, look forward to*

5 Key

a 3	c 2
b 4	d 1

6 Key

a waiting for
b expecting
c looking forward to getting
d hope you like
e expecting
f looking forward to

Speaking p144

Long turn

2 After students have read through the task, check they understand what they have to do by asking the following questions: *Student A: What do you have to do first?* (compare and contrast photos 1 and 2) *What do you have to do after that?* (say in which situation I think the most effective learning is taking place) *What does effective learning mean exactly?* (a situation in which students are learning what they are supposed to be learning) *Student B: What should you be doing while Student A is talking?* (listening carefully) *What will you do when Student A has finished speaking?* (say which of the two classrooms in the photos I'd prefer to learn in)

Monitor students as they do the task and give feedback to the class. (Did Student A complete both parts of the task? Did Student B listen well? Did Student B give good reasons for their opinion?)

Possible answer

Both photos 1 and 2 show classroom situations. In photo 1, the classroom is less formal: the students are sat around a table in a small group. In photo 2, the classroom is more formal, with all of the students facing in the same direction. The teacher is more controlling. More learning may be taking place in photo 1 where the students are more actively involved.

3 After students have read the task, check their understanding by asking similar questions to the ones you asked in task 2.

Possible answers

Both photos 3 and 4 show students studying individually. In photo 3, the student is at a desk, possibly revising or doing homework. In photo 4, the student is having one-to-one tuition with a teacher. The situation in photo 4 looks more enjoyable since the student gets more responses to his or her ideas and is less likely to get bored.

Vocabulary p145

Lead in

1 Check students understand the meaning of *compliment* (praise, an admiring comment).

Key

Describing someone as being *skinny* is not a compliment as it suggests that they don't look very healthy.

Positive or negative?

2 Key

a cheap	d fake	g pricey
b ruthless	e gossiping	h sneers
c fat	f hysterical	i old

3 Key

a reserved	e curious
b self-confident	f outgoing
c easy-going	g shy
d serious	h intelligent

Optional activity

Give students the following school report and ask them to rewrite it in a less complimentary form.

Jason has an easy-going approach to his work. He is an intelligent and self-confident young man who always completes his work very quickly. Jason is outgoing and likes to be popular. He spends a lot of time chatting with other members of the class who unfortunately may need the time to do their own work. Jason does not really understand this and simply smiles when it is pointed out to him.

(Possible answer: Jason has *a lazy* approach to his work. He is *a smart and self-satisfied* young man who always completes his work very quickly. Jason is *arrogant* and likes to be popular. He spends a lot of time *gossiping* with other members of the class who unfortunately may need the time to do their own work. Jason does not really understand this and simply *smirks* when it is pointed out to him.)

Over to you

The saying 'sticks and stones may break my bones, but words can never hurt me' suggests that although there is danger from physical violence, verbal abuse should be ignored as it can't really harm you.

Writing p146

Formal letter

1 After students have read the information, check they understand by asking the following questions: *When will you arrive for the course?* (Saturday June 30th) *Where will you arrive at?*

(Heathrow) *How will you get from the airport?* (being met by an English friend) *What kind of accommodation do you want?* (with an English family, but not with another student) *What trips are you interested in?* (London, Cambridge) *Do you have any other questions?* (When do you have to pay the fees?)

Key

a The main purpose is to answer the questions asked by the language school.
b It is necessary to include your arrival date, that you don't need to be picked up at the airport, the type of accommodation required and which trips you are interested in going on.
c The style should be formal.

2 Possible answer

Dear Ms Simpson,
Thank you for your letter which *arrived* this morning. *I'm looking forward to* coming to your school.
To answer your question about my arrival, I will be getting to Heathrow airport the day before the course, *which is* July 1. However, a friend is meeting me, so I will not need a taxi. Thank *you for being to thoughtful.*
Secondly, as regards accommodation, I would prefer to stay alone with a family. *Please do not think that I am antisocial,* but I really want to practise my English conversation.
Regarding the trips. I would like to go to London and Stratford, but not Brighton, as I studied there last year.
I have one question which is, when should I pay the course fees? Can I pay in July, or *would you prefer me to pay now?*
I am looking forward to meeting you all.
Yours sincerely,
Maria

Focusing expressions

3 Key

To answer your question about my arrival
Secondly, as regards accommodation

4 Possible answers

As far as my arrival is concerned, …
As regards my arrival, …
As for accommodation, …
Moving on to your next question about accommodation, …
Regarding trips, …
With regard to trips, …

Think, plan, write

5 After students have read the task and the information, ask the following questions: *What have you enrolled on?* (an intensive English language course) *Why?* (to help pass an important exam) *In general what does the school want to know?* (about my particular language needs; what I hope to gain) *How do you feel about grammar?* (confident) *What about conversation?* (terrible) *Which of the skills do you need most practice in?* (speaking) *What are your particular problems?* (speak too slowly; make mistakes; have a strong accent) *Why do you want to pass the exam?* (because I'm going to live in Australia) *How do you prefer to work?* (in pairs or groups) *Why?* (for the speaking practice)

6 Encourage students to refer to the Writing guide on page 162.

Overview p148

1 Key

1	than	5	the	9	been
2	Not	6	whether	10	has
3	make	7	to	11	between
4	ago	8	at	12	which

2 Key

a	I take	e	I'll tell
b	we'd go	f	had accepted
c	hadn't	g	you tell
d	you bring	h	I'd phone

3 Key

a	say	e	hope
b	speak	f	looking forward to
c	speaking	g	expect
d	tells		

An extra activity to accompany this unit and a unit test can be downloaded from the Internet at www.oup.com/elt/teacher/exams

12 Society

Introduction p149

1 Possible answer

1 This photo shows a young person involved in graffiti. It illustrates low-level crime which can be quite common and which is often associated with young people.

2 This photo shows the use of credit cards to pay for products. Credit cards can lead people into more and more debt, which can have negative effects on their lives.

3 This picture shows a young mother with a child. People having children very young can mean that they do not develop a career. Also the children may not get good care from parents who have little experience.

4 This photo shows a young man looking at vacancies in a job centre, which is where people go to look for work. This photo illustrates a negative aspect of society: unemployment.

Reading p150

Think ahead

2 Key

A a robbery, drink driving, burglary
  b having a gun pointed at his head
  c actor
B a vandalism
  b his probation officer
  c US senator
C a assault
  b teachers and counsellors
  c criminal defence lawyer
D a attempted murder
  b being arrested for attempted murder
  c lawyer
E a assaulting a teacher
  b being sent to an alternative school rather than jail
  c Olympic long jumper

Multiple matching

3 You may like to check that students understand the meaning of these words: *juvenile* (young person, not subject to adult laws), *role model* (somebody who influences the behaviour of others – usually young people), *rival* (opposition), *transition* (change), *stable* (steady), *filed* (made), *juvenile detention centre* (kind of prison for young people), *short fuse* (short temper; able to get angry very easily), *assaulting* (attacking), *delinquents* (young people who get in trouble with the law). Ask students to underline the part of the text which gives the reason for B being the correct answer for the example (made up his lost years of education). Encourage students to do the same as they continue through the task in order to justify their answers.

Key

1	A	9,10	B/C
2,3	C/D	11	E
4	B	12,13	B/D
5,6	A/C	14	C
7,8	D/E	15	A

Crime vocabulary

4 Key

a vandalism   d shoplifting
b drink-driving   e hooligans
c mugger   f burglary

5 Point out the difference between *steal* and *rob*: you steal things, but you rob a person or a place.

Key

a has been robbed; was stolen
b being stolen
c 've been robbed
d stealing
e stole
f were stolen

Grammar and practice p152

Probability and possibility

1 Key

a might b can't c must

2 Key

a must b can't c might

3 Key

a past c future
b present d present

4 Encourage students to refer to the Grammar reference on page 190.

Key

a *have* + past participle
b *be* + *-ing*
c infinitive without *to*
d infinitive without *to*

Other structures with similar meanings:
must: probably, bound to
can't: probably not
might: maybe, perhaps, possibly

5 Key

a must/might, can't have been/might not have been
b can't have said
c can't have heard
d must be, could/might be
e can't have left
f must have got
g might have been wearing
h must have left
i can't have forgotten, must have happened, could/might have broken down
j must have taken

6 Key

a in his own home
b on Friday evening
c He was shot once in the head.
d money
e three

7 Key

Simon Prince
Relationship to Miller	*neighbour*
Marital status	*divorced*
Possible motive	*money*
Bad habits	*drinking, gambling*

Margaret McKenzie
Relationship to Miller	*housekeeper*
Marital status	*married (husband in prison)*
Possible motive	*disliked employer, money*
Bad habits	*smoking*

Timothy Carlyle
Relationship to Miller	*best friend*
Marital status	*single*
Possible motive	*money, jealousy*
Bad habits	*drinking*

Audioscript

Officer	How's the Miller Case going, Inspector?
Inspector	Well, Ma'am ... I've just finished interviewing our three main suspects. That's Simon Prince, Margaret McKenzie and Timothy Carlyle. There was no forced entry to the house, no broken windows or doors, so we concluded that the murderer and the victim must have known each other.
Officer	Tell me about Prince. He found the body, didn't he?
Inspector	That's right and contacted us. He heard the shot. He's Miller's neighbour and has known him for years.
Officer	What's his financial situation?
Inspector	He was a financial director until two years ago. He lost his job and things have gone very wrong for him since. He's got a lot of debts.
Officer	So, we have a motive – money. What else do we know about him?
Inspector	He's got a few bad habits. He's a heavy drinker. He has a gambling problem. His wife divorced him last year. He's in quite a state – unshaven, unwashed, no smart clothes.
Officer	Right ... one unhappy man. What about Margaret McKenzie?

Inspector	She's the housekeeper. She worked for Miller for about three years. I got the impression she didn't like him much. I don't think her wages were very high and she's got three children.
Officer	Husband?
Inspector	In prison – for burglary – he's a master at blowing up safes, apparently.
Officer	Interesting … Miller's safe was blown, wasn't it?
Inspector	That's right.
Officer	OK. Anything else? Does she have any bad habits? Drinking? Drugs?
Inspector	None that we know about. Well, she smokes cigarettes, but that's about all.
Officer	Timothy Carlyle?
Inspector	He was Miller's best friend. They'd known each other for years. He's got a reasonable job in a bank, but I don't think he earns a lot, so perhaps money could have been a motive …
Officer	… or jealousy … of a successful friend?
Inspector	Maybe.
Officer	Married or single?
Inspector	Single and very presentable looking – always very smart, shirt and tie, hat and briefcase.
Officer	Seeing anyone?
Inspector	Not that he'd admit to, although I get the feeling that he was lying when I asked him that question.
Officer	Interesting … Why would he lie about that? What about bad habits?
Inspector	He drinks a bit, I think. Nothing serious.

Possible answers

Somebody must have been drinking whisky because there are two glasses on the table and an open bottle.

The murderer must have been a smoker because there is an unfinished cigarette in the ashtray.

The murderer must have known where the safe was because the picture has been removed.

The murderer might have been a man because there is a man's hat left on the table, or the murderer could have been a woman because a woman's scarf has been left on the armchair.

9 Audioscript

Officer	Congratulations, Inspector. I hear you've made an arrest.
Inspector	That's right.
Officer	Perhaps you could fill me in?
Inspector	Of course. We made a detailed study of the crime scene. There were two glasses on the coffee table and a half empty bottle of whisky. This suggested that the victim must have known his murderer.
Officer	And that the murderer was a drinker.
Inspector	That's right. This ruled out McKenzie and pointed to either Prince or Carlyle who both drink. There was, however, a cigarette in the ashtray. We found no cigarettes belonging to Miller in the house, so we assume he was a non-smoker. The only smoker amongst our suspects is McKenzie. We also found a lady's scarf on one of the chairs again pointing to the housekeeper. Also the Hoover was still in the room and it was plugged in! That said to me she must have been in the house at the time of the murder otherwise it would have been put away.
Officer	Then of course there was the fact that explosives were used …
Inspector	… and McKenzie's husband is in prison for using explosives.
Officer	So you arrested Margaret McKenzie.
Inspector	Yes, we did. But … there's something else …
Officer	The whisky glasses …
Inspector	… and the hat. There was a man's hat on the table.
Officer	Simon Prince's?
Inspector	No … I decided it can't have been his … it was too smart.
Officer	Timothy Carlyle?
Inspector	That's right. He and McKenzie were in it together … for the money.

Listening p154

Lead in

2 Possible answer

People are encouraged through advertising to want more and more items such as fast cars, big houses, clothes and expensive holidays. Banks often give credit too easily. These factors can cause people to get into debt or even to commit crimes. Worry about money can also cause stress which can lead to problems within families.

Multiple matching

3 Make sure students read the options before they listen to the recording.

Key

Speaker 1	C	Speaker 4	D
Speaker 2	F	Speaker 5	B
Speaker 3	A		

Extra letter: E

Audioscript

Speaker 1 For some people it's a harmless enough activity. **They can have the odd bet, buy the occasional lottery ticket and it doesn't do them any harm.** But for me it was much more than that. It was like an obsession; it ended up controlling me rather than the other way round. **Of course, you always think you're going to win**; you never think you're going to lose. Fortunately, I was one of the lucky ones; I got help and my family were very supportive. And I don't have a problem with it any more ... I don't think it's considered a problem by society in the same way that alcoholism is, for example, but I think it should be. It can be just as serious a problem as being an alcoholic.

Speaker 2 Some people say that drugs are largely to blame and that if they legalised hard drugs it would make a huge difference to the figures, but not everyone who breaks the law is a drug addict. That wasn't what drove me to it. It was simply a case of getting more money. All the activities I've been involved in are basically ways of making a living. **OK, they're easy ways of making a living, and I suppose most people would say that they were illegal, but unless I get caught, I've got no intention of doing an ordinary job. There's just not enough money in it.**

Speaker 3 When I was at university, **I took out a loan to help me pay my way and by the time I graduated I owed £4,000.** To be honest, I wasn't really bothered at first as I expected to get a good job straight away and be able to pay it back quite quickly. However, I still haven't got a proper job and now I owe £3,000 on my credit cards on top of the bank loan, and I've got absolutely no idea what I'm going to do. I think most people my age owe money, though maybe not as much as me. It's partly my fault, but I think credit card companies and banks are responsible as well. It's just too easy to get credit nowadays.

Speaker 4 Money was always a problem. When I met John he had a good job but he lost it shortly after we got married. However, I had a job and we thought we could make ends meet. Then I got pregnant and had to give up work to look after the baby. John still couldn't find a job and by this time there was another one on the way. We couldn't afford to buy nice things for the kids or go out or do anything. That's when we started arguing and from then on things just got worse. **In the end there was nothing there and we split up. We got divorced last year.** I think if we hadn't had money problems, we might still be together.

Speaker 5 If you owe money you worry about how on earth you are going to pay it back. If you can't afford to buy your kids presents for Christmas you get stressed and upset. Even when you've got enough money, you think you need more. You get caught up in the rat race, end up working too hard, and **if you don't do something about it you can find yourself having a heart attack when you're still in your forties, just like I did.** Now I realise there are far more important things in life than money. Money, whether we have it or we don't, just causes problems.

Speaking p155

Lead in

1 Possible answers

a The speaker considers the person in question is wearing something ridiculous or has done something ridiculous to their appearance.

b The speaker thinks the person in question needs to be admonished for their bad behaviour or laziness.

c The speaker thinks the person in question feels she's better than other people.

d The speaker is directing this comment at somebody who is behaving in an immature way.

e The speaker thinks the person in question is wearing clothes that are too young for her.

2 Possible answers

1 Many people distrust homeless people, often making the assumption that they are drug addicts or violent in some way.

2 Although many people admire rich people and would like to be rich, rich people are also disliked by some people.

3 The photo shows a positive image of a disabled person taking part in sport. Although there is more acceptance of disabled people in today's society, they are not always treated equally. They sometimes have difficulties with access in public places.

4 This photo shows an elderly person taking part in a race. Some people consider that elderly people have nothing left to contribute to society. They are often given poor pensions and bad housing and are treated in a patronising way by the media and younger people.

Long turn

3 Make sure each student understands what they have to do. While students are doing the task, monitor their discussions and give feedback to the class about their performance. (Did they compare and contrast the photos effectively? Did they speak for a minute when doing so? Did they give reasons for their opinions? Did they listen to each other?)

Possible answers

Photo 1 shows someone who is homeless, possibly asking for money from people walking by but being ignored. Photo 2 shows someone who is obviously rich from her clothes and the way she looks, with someone paying her lots of attention. Being rich doesn't necessarily make you happy, but it may solve a lot of problems. Nevertheless, many people believe they could be happy if they were rich.

Photos 3 and 4 both show people taking part in sporting events. The competitions are different, however. The person in Photo 3 is much younger, but is handicapped – this person is taking part in a wheelchair race. The person in Photo 4 is quite old but seems to be healthy. I admire both people but possibly the wheelchair athlete more because they have overcome a greater physical difficulty.

Grammar and practice p156

Lead in

1 Possible answers

a If you add the first two figures of your age multiply by the second then divide by the first … it won't change a thing you'll still be a year older.

b You know you're getting on when someone gives you a cake … and you can't see it for the candles.

c The secret of staying young is the careful use of make-up … just make up an age and stick to it.

The cards show that people often make jokes about getting older and that older people are teased about their appearance and their memory.

Articles

2 Key

1 a	7 a	13 an
2 —	8 an	14 a
3 —	9 —	15 the
4 the	10 The	16 the
5 the	11 the	17 —
6 —	12 a	

Encourage students to refer to the Grammar reference on p191.

Vocabulary p157

Multiple-choice cloze

3 Key

a every two years
b £220 million
c comedians and ordinary people

4 Key

1 D	5 B	9 D
2 C	6 C	10 A
3 A	7 A	11 B
4 C	8 A	12 D

When students have completed the task, check they understand the meaning of these words: *set up* (started), *get something across* (give a message to people, explain something), *unites* (brings people together), *all walks of life* (different kinds of people), *take over* (take charge), *hard-hitting* (usually shocking and having a serious impact on people), *donations* (money given to charity).

Writing p158

Lead in

1 Possible answers

Ways of raising money: the lottery; sponsored events; holding an international concert; collecting money; asking for donations; holding fêtes or fairs; charity shops; fundraising events on TV.

a The lottery is likely to raise the most money on a regular basis, although a concert or an evening of fundraising by celebrities on TV would raise the most in one go.

b Collecting money in the street would probably be the easiest to organise.

Report

2 Key

a formal

b suggestions on how to raise money to buy the new equipment

c yes

3 When students have read the report, ask them to make comments about its organisation and style. (It is headed at the beginning: To/From/Subject. The main body is divided into two paragraphs. Each paragraph has an underlined heading – fund-raising activities and recommendation.)

Key

a two – organise a sponsored race, charge an entrance fee for the next end-of-year concert

4 Key

Since all the proceeds would go to the hospital I am certain our parents would be happy to contribute.

5 Possible answers

a You could collect money in the town centre on a Saturday, which is the busiest time.

b We collected a lot of money so that the hospital was able to buy the equipment it needed.

c They were able to buy a kidney dialysis machine in addition to some toys.

d Despite the weather being very bad, people still collected a lot of money.

e As the concert was a huge success, we're going to organise another one next year.

f Children donated both toys they don't play with any more and books they don't read any more.

g Not only was the sponsored ride very enjoyable, but it also raised a lot of money.

h As well as offering a prize of a dinner for two, a local restaurant also gave a donation to the hospital.

i Although the school raised £500, it wasn't enough to buy the equipment.

j The head teacher thanked all the students who had helped to make the event a success.

Think, plan, write

6 Check students have understood the task by asking the following questions: *Who is the council worried about?* (young people who get into trouble because they are bored) *What do they plan to do about it?* (give out information about cheap or free activities in the area) *What do they want you to do?* (make suggestions about what activities are available)

9 Encourage students to refer to the Writing guide on page 169.

Overview p160

1 Key

1 was arrested for vandalising
2 he owed his success to
3 to let his mother hit
4 was interested in helping
5 must have heard
6 might not have wanted
7 that the elderly keep/for the elderly to keep
8 was such a successful concert

2 Key

a		b	
1	The	1	—
2	—	2	—
3	a	3	a
4	—	4	the
5	—	5	a
6	A/The	6	the
7	the	7	The
8	a	8	the
9	the		
10	the		

An extra activity to accompany this unit, a unit test and Progress Test 3 (Units 9–12) can be downloaded from the Internet at www.oup.com/elt/teacher/exams

What is oxfordenglishtesting.com?

- It's a website that gives students of English access to interactive practice tests.
- It's where students who have bought OUP Workbook Resource Packs can access online practice tests included in the Pack, and buy more if they wish.

The website will become a gateway for all sorts of English tests available to both students and institutions.

You can register on oxfordenglishtesting.com and try a free sample test to see how it works. A demo is also available from your local OUP office.

What is on the Student's Workbook MultiROM?

The MultiROM has two parts.
- Students can listen to the audio material that accompanies the Workbook by playing the MultiROM in an audio CD player, or in a media player on their computer.
- Students can also access one or two practice tests online with the MultiROM.

More about the tests

The online practice tests reflect what happens in the real exam, in the same way as printed practice tests from Oxford University Press. They include every paper and question that a student will find in the real exam.

With the exception of the Speaking Test, students do not print the tests in order to do them. They take them online and most questions are marked automatically online. In addition, there are help features that students can use. These include dictionary look-up, exam tips, the ability to mark and change individual answers, and get feedback on answers. See test features on the page opposite for more details.

Students have access to each test for three months before they must submit it for final marking. They can choose to do parts of the test, or the whole test at any time during that period. Students can monitor their progress via the **Test Overview** which records questions not attempted, attempted but not marked, questions that cannot be marked online, and right and wrong answers. Students can also print the **Test Overview** and **Results** page.

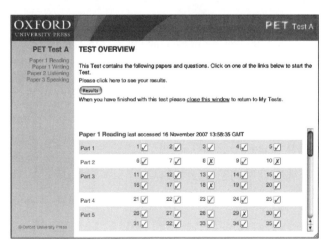

Writing and Speaking papers

The website cannot automatically mark the Writing essay questions and Speaking papers online. The default result will exclude these papers. The result the students see includes totals for each of the parts and a percentage. It also gives an indication as to whether the score is equivalent to a pass or not. Obviously this is a practice test not the real exam and the result is only an indication of what students might achieve in a real exam.

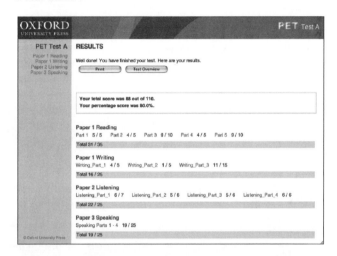

There are *sample answers* for Writing questions which give students an idea of what is expected of them. If you want students to enter a score for essay questions, they can print their essay, or email it to you so that you can mark it. They can then enter their marks into the **Results** page on the website. Their final score will then be adjusted to take the marks into account.

Students get sample Speaking papers and *Useful language* to help them practise offline. The Speaking paper can be printed from the **My tests** page. If you want you can conduct the Speaking Test with students and they can enter their marks into the **Results** page on the website. Their final score will then be adjusted to take the marks into account.

Tests for purchase by teachers and institutions

From September 2008, teachers and institutions will be able to buy and administer practice tests for their students. The tests will be different to those available to students via Workbook Resource Packs or purchased by students online. Teachers will be able to set the tests in practice or test mode, and will be able to record students' results. There will also be a placement test that can be used to determine students' level of English.

For more information go www.oup.com/elt.

There is also a list of Frequently Asked Questions (FAQs) on the website. Go to www.oxfordenglishtesting.com, click on any link to register and then go to the **Support** tab.

What are the features of the test?

Exam tips	There is a tip on how to answer every question.
Dictionary look-up	Students can look up the meaning of any word in the practice test. They just double click it and a definition will pop up. They will need to have pop-up windows enabled.
Instant marking and feedback	When a student has answered a question, they can mark it straight away to see whether they got it right. If the answer was wrong, they can get feedback to find out why it was wrong.
Change your answer or try again	Students can then go back and have another go as many times as they like. Understanding why they answered a question incorrectly helps them think more clearly about a similar question next time.
Save and come back later	Students don't have to complete a Paper in one go. When they log out it saves what they've done. They can come back to it at any time. Students have 90 days before they have to submit the practice test for final marking. The **My tests** page tells students how many days they have left to access the test.
Mark individual answers, a part, a paper or the whole test	However much students have done of the practice test, they can mark it and see how well they're doing.
Audio scripts	These are available for all parts of the Listening test. Reading the audio script will help students understand any areas they didn't understand when they were listening to them.
Sample answers for essay questions in the Writing paper	Students can see *sample answers* after they've written their own. They've been written by real students, and will give them a good idea of what's expected. The essay they write will not be marked automatically. If you would like to mark your student's essay, tell them and they can either print it off to give to you, or email it to you. When you've marked it, they can enter the mark on their **Results** page. It does not matter if they do not enter a mark for the essay. The final marks will be adjusted to take that into account.
Useful phrases for the Speaking paper	Students get sample Speaking papers and *Useful language* to help them practise offline. If you want to assess your students they can print the Speaking paper from the **My tests** page, and ask you to do the Speaking paper with them. As with the Writing paper, you can give them a mark and they can enter the mark on the **Results** page. However, if you don't, their final marks will be adjusted to take that into account.
Results page	Remember this is a practice test not the real exam. Students will see their score by paper and part and as a percentage. This will only be an indication as to whether their score is equivalent to a pass or not.
Try a sample test first	You can try out a short version of a practice test yourself. Go to oxfordenglishtesting. com and click on **Try**. You can also ask your local OUP office for a demo.
Buy more practice tests	To get even more practice, students can buy more tests on oxfordenglishtesting.com